To George with my
best wishes.

Vincent Drago

3 Nov. 2010

D1032065

THE SIGHTS OF ROME

Uncovering the legends and curiosities of the Eternal City

by Vincent O. Drago

Copyright © 2010, Vincent Drago

ISBN: 978-0-692-00630-6

Library of Congress Control Number: 2009911022

All rights reserved. No part of this book may be reproduced or transmitted in any form
or by any means, electronic or mechanical, including photocopying, recording, or
by information storage and retrieval systems, without the written permission of the
publisher, except by a reviewer who may quote brief passages in a review.

Printed in the United States of America

FOREWORD

I thought I knew Rome until I had occasion to spend some time on the streets of the Eternal City with Vincent Drago, a true scholar of the Latin language and Roman history. Vince's knowledge and understanding of Rome goes far beyond what is contained in the best guidebooks. He has uncovered the mysteries and secrets behind every architectural structure, monument, statue and painting. He speaks of emperors, artists and popes as if they were his friends. As a matter of fact, the men and women who made Roman history *are* Vince's friends, dear to his heart. That is why he chose to make the Eternal City his home.

Vincent Drago's Sights of Rome brings the City alive with photographs and curious information. He puts flesh, blood and bones on people, places and things we never noticed. He unlocks the curious details in the most ordinary sight of Rome. After my numerous visits to Rome over the past thirty-eight years, Vincent's Sights of Rome enables me to appreciate the City from a totally enlightened perspective. That is why I encouraged him to put his work in book form. The Scholar presents his sights and insights in a straight forward style without excessive detail. I am grateful to Vincent Drago for sharing his love and in-depth understanding of the Eternal City.

Paul V. Canonici

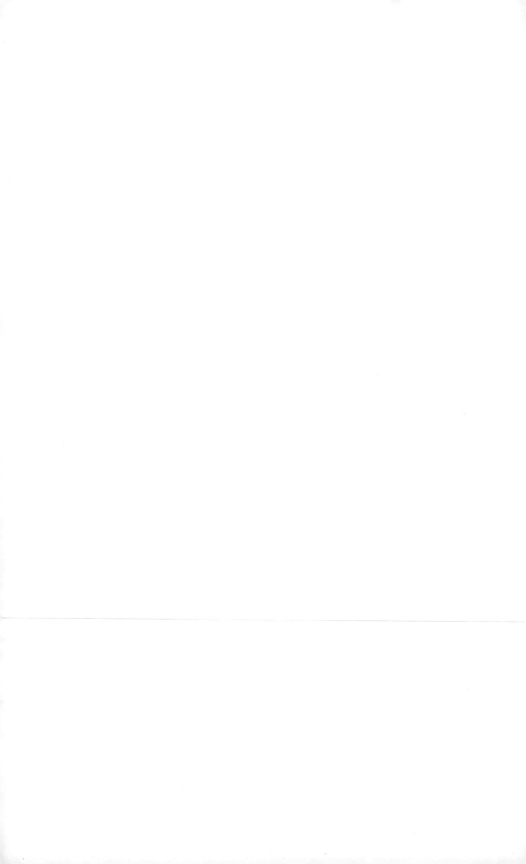

INTRODUCTION

In 1898, Anthony (Tony) Drago, age 18, boarded the merchant and passenger ship Montebello and sailed from his native Palermo, Sicily to the United States, eventually settling in New Iberia, Louisiana. Young Tony was destined never again to set foot in his native land. Although he lived on an island, in the small town of Alia, just a short distance from the port of Palermo, Tony had never even seen the sea until the day he left that little town and traveled the few miles to Palermo to board the Montebello. One hundred and two years later, in August of the year 2000, Tony's grandson, Vincent, age 60, boarded a plane that would take him to Italy to spend his retirement years in Rome. After two generations it was immigration in reverse!

That flight in 2000 was by no means my first trip to Italy. I had logged some fifteen round trips beginning in 1965, including a visit to Alia, my grandfather's birthplace. But this time it was different. This time the ticket was one-way. This time I was going to stay. It was definitely a different feeling. Rome, the Eternal City! It had always been special to me, and it seemed a perfect fit for one who had spent over thirty-five years teaching Latin. Although it is not a complete return to my Sicilian roots, it is close enough.

After a few years in Rome I began to feel the need to put something in writing as a way of sharing with family and friends some of the beauty and history of this marvelous city. But write what? Where to start? There is so much here that it literally overwhelms you. In the end I chose not one place, but dozens of places and subjects, in the form of short descriptions which I call *The Sights of Rome*. In the *Sights*, I try to convey my own love and passion for this exciting city, its history, its art, its people and its customs.

By way of explanation, the chapters in this book are arranged alphabetically by topic. In this way they can be read in any order because they are not interdependent. All of them have purposefully been kept relatively short, which allows the reader to finish a complete description in a matter of minutes. Of course this brevity also means that these descriptions are not scholarly pieces, nor are they intended to be in-depth treatments of the topics. They are more what I would call "verbal snapshots", to be read leisurely and for pure pleasure. So my hope is that you will enjoy reading about the Eternal City as much as I have enjoyed writing about it. The photographs in this book are by the author unless otherwise indicated.

CONTENTS

The spectacular Acqua Paola fountain on the Janiculum hill marks
the end of a Roman aqueduct.

Chapter 1

The Acqua Paola Fountain
Recycling to the max!

Paul V Borghese. He gave us the
Acqua Paola fountain.

It would be a difficult task for me to choose my favorite fountain in Rome, but surely the *Acqua Paola* on the **Janiculum hill** would be among my first choices. Not only is this fountain a beautiful work of **seventeenth-century baroque architecture**, but it also sits on a terrace which provides a breathtaking **panoramic view of Rome**. The fountain is so large (30 meters high) that it looks more like the façade of a building rather than a fountain. As a result the Romans have nicknamed it *il fontanone* (the big fountain). It underwent an extensive **two-year restoration** a few years ago, the result of which was nothing short of spectacular.

Il fontanone has a long and interesting history which goes back to the **early second century A.D.** In the year 109 the **emperor Trajan** built an **aqueduct** to bring water from Lake Bracciano, 64 kilometers northwest of Rome, to the Janiculum hill overlooking the city. The imperial aqueduct eventually fell into disrepair, but was restored and reconstructed in the seventh century by **Pope Honorius I (625-638)**, and was further restored by **Paul V Borghese (1605-1621)**, who enlarged it to provide water to the nearby areas of **Trastevere** and the **Vatican**. The large inscription on the face of the fountain refers to this restoration and enlargement of the imperial aqueducts by the Borghese pope.

PAULUS QUINTUS PONTIFEX MAXIMUS
AQUAM IN AGRO BRACCIANENSI
SALUBERRIMIS E FONTIBUS COLLECTAM
VETERIBUS AQUAE ALSIETINAE DUCTIBUS RESTITUTIS
NOVISQUE ADDITIS
XXXV AB MILLIARIO DUXIT

ANNO DOMINI MDCXII PONTIFICATUS SUI SEPTIMO

(Paul V, Supreme Pontiff, brought water, collected from very healthy springs, from the thirty-fifth milestone in the field of Bracciano, having restored the ancient Alsietina aqueducts and having added new ones, in the year of the Lord 1612, the seventh of his pontificate)

A curiosity

• There is a **historical inaccuracy** in the inscription. It states that the ancient *Alsietina* aqueducts were restored, when in fact it was the *Trajan* aqueduct. The mistake is understandable because the terminus of the Trajan aqueduct was unknown at the time the inscription was made.

Once he had restored the aqueducts Paul V commissioned **Giovanni Fontana** and **Flaminio Ponzio** to build the fountain, which they did, using **recycled marble** from the Forum of Nerva. The decorations, like the inscription, are obviously intended to glorify the pope. At the top of the structure, below the cross, two angels flank the pope's Borghese family **coat of arms** (the eagle and the dragon), below which is the inscription. Eagles and dragons, reflecting the papal coat of arms, are seen in various places on the fountain.

A curiosity

• This is the same pope (Paul V Borghese), the same coat of arms (eagle and dragon) and the same year (1612) which are seen across the façade of **St. Peter's Basilica**, which was completed in the same year as the fountain.

Below the massive inscription are **six columns**, all of which were recycled from the old St. Peter's Basilica built by the **emperor Constantine** in the **fourth century**. The four middle ones are made of **red granite** and are slightly larger than the two end ones which are made of **grey granite**. The four red granite columns come from the gate in front of the quadriporticus of the old basilica, while the two grey ones are from the façade. The columns are separating **five arches**, three large ones in the middle and two smaller ones on either side.

The water originally flowed out from openings in the five arches into five separate basins below, but in **1690** those basins were rearranged by **Carlo Fontana** to create one large **semicircular basin** into which the water gushes from the three large center openings. A smaller flow of water falls from the mouth of a dragon in the two side arches. Then in **1698** the basin was enclosed by a row of **waist-high columns** in front, connected to one another by iron bars to prevent the carriage drivers from watering their horses in the fountain. Today the barrier serves just as well to prevent **wild Roman drivers** from crashing into the fountain as they roar around the semicircle!

A curiosity

• When the water was first turned on in a **trial run** after the restoration of the aqueduct in **1610**, the rush of water was much stronger than anticipated, causing

major flooding in all of Trastevere at the bottom of the hill. Serious adjustments to the flow had to be made.

You will notice either **soldiers** or **carabinieri** (national military police) patroling in the immediate area of the fountain. They are there to provide security for the residence of the **Spanish ambassador to Italy** which is just across the street from the fountain. And if you look just up the street to the left of the fountain you will see another contingent of carabinieri across the street from a building which flies the **American flag**. This is the residence of the **American ambassador to the Vatican**.

A frontal view of the *Acqua Paola* fountain.

The façade and dome of *Sant'Ivo alla Sapienza*. (Photo by Hugh Lee)

Chapter 2

The Barberini Bee Stings Again
Urban VIII and Borromini

A close-up of the unique spiral dome.

Among the great architects who literally changed the landscape of Rome was **Francesco Borromini (1599-1667)**. Perhaps his great misfortune was to be a contemporary and adversary of **Gian Lorenzo Bernini (1598-1680)**. Borromini spent most of his professional life in the shadow of his better-known rival. His tragic **suicide** on **August 2, 1667**, was due at least partially to his despair over that rivalry. Borromini, however, left us some remarkable and unique architectural wonders in the Eternal City, not the least of which is the little **Church of Sant'Ivo alla Sapienza**, just across the street from **Piazza Navona**.

The name of the church, Sant'Ivo alla Sapienza, requires some explanation. The church was built between **1642 and 1666** as the chapel of the **University of Rome**, which is called **La Sapienza** (wisdom). So the church is really named "Sant'Ivo at the University of Rome".

Curiosities

• The University of Rome is one of the oldest universities in Europe, having been founded by **Boniface VIII in 1303**. It continued to operate in this location until **1935** when it was relocated to larger quarters in the **San Lorenzo** neighborhood near **Stazione Termini**, Rome's major train station.

• But what about the other part of the church's name? Why was it dedicated to the little-known **Saint Ivo**? Born in Brittany in **1253**, Ivo was a well-known and respected scholar, theologian and Canon lawyer. He died in **1303**, the year the University was founded, so the decision to dedicate the church to him was quite appropriate.

Now let's get to the somewhat **odd title** of this chapter: *The Barberini Bee Stings Again*. Borromini received the commission to design the church from **Urban VIII Barberini (1623-1644)**. Urban, however, didn't live to see the church completed; it was finished and dedicated under another pope, **Alexander VII Chigi (1655-1667)**. That's why we see in various places in and on the building the **stars and mounds** which reflect the **coat of arms** of the Chigi pope.

Borromini, however, wanted to honor Urban VIII, the pope who had awarded him the commission to build the church, and he did this in a clever and unique manner. As everybody in the world knows, the coat of arms of the

Barberini pope, which seems to be ubiquitous in Rome, is decorated with **three bees**. Well, look at the unusual shape of the dome of Sant'Ivo. Borromini designed it in a beautiful **spiral shape**, tapering off at the peak, so that anyone looking at it should be reminded of a **bee's stinger**, thus recalling the bees on Urban VIII's coat of arms! The spiral dome of Sant'Ivo has become another of Rome's celebrated landmarks. It is the only one of its kind in the city and can be seen from as far away as the **Janiculum hill.**

There are certain characteristics which can help you discover if the building or church you are looking at in Rome is a work of Borromini. For example, nothing appears flat; everything seems to be moving, either **advancing** toward you or **receding** away from you (convex and concave). Also, look for **circles and triangles** in Borromini-designed buildings, the circles perhaps representing the **infinity of God** and the triangles the **Holy Trinity**.

The coat of arms of Urban VIII.

The Fountain of the Four Rivers in Piazza Navona.

Chapter 3

Bernini, Borromini, Innocent X
Whose fountain is it, really?

A close-up of the watery masterpiece.

In the late sixteenth century, **Gregory XIII Boncompagni (1572-1585)** awarded to **Giacomo Della Porta** the commission to design a fountain, now known as the **Fontana del Moro**, at the southern end of **Piazza Navona**. In the center of the piazza Della Porta placed a simple rectangular **drinking trough** for horses and donkeys. About 75 years later, **Innocent X Pamphili (1644-1655)**, whose family palace by then graced the southeastern side of the piazza, decided that the animal trough simply had to go and that a glorious fountain should rise in its place, something worthy of the noble Pamphili family. This papal decision would produce, after many controversies, the magnificent **Fountain of the Four Rivers**.

Many people are surprised to learn that it was **Borromini, not Bernini**, who suggested to Innocent that the theme of the fountain should be four great rivers—the **Danube, Ganges, Nile** and **Rio Della Plata**—representing the four continents of the known world: Europe, Asia, Africa and the Americas. The pope approved Borromini's plan for the fountain and he also decided that its decoration should include an **ancient obelisk** which the Romans had cut in Egypt and transported to Rome in the first century A.D. The obelisk had recently been found in pieces in the **Circus of Maxentius** on the Appian Way. The pontiff ordered that it be reassembled and incorporated into the fountain.

A curiosity

• The obelisk very nearly ended up in **Great Britain** rather than in Rome's Piazza Navona. An Englishman, **William Petty**, saw the obelisk, in pieces in the Circus of Maxentius in 1636. He immediately understood its poten- tial **economic value** and he purchased it from the pontifical administration. Petty intended to have it transported to England where he had already found a buyer. When **Urban VIII Barberini (1623-1644)** learned of the Englishman's plans, he blocked the exportation of the obelisk. A generation later it was immortalized as part of the fountain.

Several artists, including Borromini, were invited to submit a design for the fountain, using Borromini's theme of the four rivers. Conspicuous by his absence from this list was Bernini whom Innocent shunned because of the artist's close relationship with the **Barberini family** of his predecessor, Urban

VIII. The Barberini and Pamphili families were fierce rivals, and after Innocent became pope, Bernini was excluded from all the prestigious **papal commissions**.

Borromini had already designed the channel which would bring water from the **Acqua Vergine aqueduct** to Piazza Navona to provide a flow of water for the fountain. And, as we know, the theme of the four rivers was his idea as well. Hence everyone, including Borromini himself, presumed that he would receive the commission. Innocent, however, was not impressed with any of the designs submitted, not even Borromini's. So for the time being no action was taken to build the fountain.

Curiosities

•   How Bernini eventually got back into the **good graces** of the pope and "stole" the commission from Borromini is a fascinating footnote to the history of the fountain. Apparently it was **Prince Nicolò Ludovisi**, a friend of Bernini, who masterminded the artist's return to papal favor. Ludovisi persuaded his friend to design and build a model of the fountain, even though he had not been asked to do so by the pope. Bernini agreed and sent his finished model to Ludovisi, who then had it brought to the Pamphili palace in Piazza Navona. It was set up in a room of the palace where Innocent would be sure to see it.

•   When the pontiff walked through that room and saw the model, it was **love at first sight**! Without knowing who had designed it, the pope was very enthusiastic about the model and praised it to the heavens. When he was told who the designer was, he put aside his grudge, summoned Bernini to his presence and awarded him the commission to build the fountain. The date was **August 15, 1647**. Borromini, of course, took this turn of events hard, and as a protest he walked off the job of another papal commission he was working on, the restyling of the **Basilica of San Giovanni in Laterano**, the pope's cathedral church.

Bernini went to work on the fountain, the cost of which soared well beyond original estimates (A problem which building projects in our times seem to have inherited!). The extravagant expenditures for a fountain while much of the population of Rome was living in abject poverty and in homes without running water prompted the following **satirical graffito** which soon appeared in the piazza on a wall near the fountain:

> *Noi volemo altro che guglie e fontane;*
> *pane volemo, pane, pane, pane.*
> (We want other than obelisks and fountains;
> it's bread we want, bread, bread, bread.)

In **June of 1651** the work was completed, just four years after Bernini had received the commission. It was time to remove the scaffolding for the **official dedication**. The pope himself came to inspect the fountain up close before the water would be turned on. Bernini, however, informed him that it was not yet possible to start the flow of water. Innocent was extremely disappointed to hear this and he turned his back on the fountain and started to walk away, a little upset with his architect.

It was just what the **master showman**, Bernini, had been waiting for. At that moment he gave a signal that the water be turned on. The roaring sound of the sudden rush of water caused the pope to turn around, and there before his eyes was the fountain in all its watery grandeur. Innocent was said to have been pleased, not only with the fountain itself, but with the **dramatic and spectacular manner** in which Bernini had presented it to him.

Today, **over 350 years later**, thousands of people every day continue to admire the genius of Bernini. But let's not forget to give Borromini the credit for the **brilliant idea** of the four rivers theme of the fountain.

A close-up of the Ganges river statue. (Photo by Gianfranco Mandas)

A close-up of the Danube river statue.

Giacomo Della Porta designed *La Fontana del Moro* in the 1500's in Piazza Navona. Bernini adapted it in the 1600's.

Santa Maria in Cosmedin, the medieval church which is home to the *Bocca della Verità* .

Chapter 4

Bocca della Verità
Don't tell a lie!

The *Bocca della Verità*,
the mouth of truth.

Just about every time I go past the church of **Santa Maria in Cosmedin** I see a long line of people in the portico of the church. They are standing in line, not to enter this magnificent medieval church, but to get their picture taken as they put their hand into the **Bocca della Verità**, the mouth of truth.

This name is given to a large circular disc in the form of a human face with its mouth wide open. It is, in fact, an **ancient Roman drain cover**, which was set up in the portico of the church in the mid-seventeenth century. It has nothing to do with religion and is totally extraneous to the church. It is there simply for decoration, and for the amusement of tourists.

A curiosity

• So what attracts people to come to the atrium of this church and stick their hand into the open mouth of an ancient drain cover? Well, the legend says that the mouth will close on the hand of the person who perjures himself while his hand is inside it.

No one knows when this legend began, but there is an accompanying **legendary story** which tells us why the *Bocca* ceased to perform its gruesome task. (As far as we know, no tourist has lost his hand in the mouth **in modern times**)! According to the legend, the wife of a wealthy patrician Roman was accused of adultery. The husband, not trusting his wife's denial of the charge, decided to put her to the test of the *Bocca della Verità*.

At the appointed time for the test, a large crowd was on hand to witness this dramatic event. Suddenly, out of the crowd of onlookers burst a man raving like a madman. In reality, however, **he was the woman's lover**! The "madman" ran up to the woman, embraced her and kissed her passionately. The crowd, shocked and indignant at the man's action, was ready to lynch him, but the woman interceded for him, saying he was obviously insane and he should just be pitied.

After the incident of the madman, the woman placed her hand in the mouth and swore the following oath:

I swear that no man has ever embraced and kissed me other than my husband . . . and that madman we just saw.

The crowd stood in silence, eagerly anticipating the snapping shut of the mouth. But the mouth remained open, and the woman's hand remained intact, to the great relief and satisfaction of her husband. The *Bocca della Verità*, however, had been tricked by the cleverness of the woman and her lover, and from that time on, **the spell was ended** and the mouth never again performed its judicial function!

Nothing brought more publicity to this legend than the 1950's movie **Roman Holiday**, starring Gregory Peck and Audrey Hepburn. Who can forget the famous scene of Peck in front of the *Bocca della Verità* pretending that his hand had been chopped off, leaving Hepburn screaming in terror? Posters of the scene are still sold today all over Rome.

The proper technique of the pose with hand in the *Bocca*.

The Colosseum seen from atop the Victor Emmanuel monument.

Chapter 5

The Colosseum
As long as it stands . . .

The exterior of the Colosseum.

The most famous of Rome's ancient monuments, and the most visited in modern times at **13,000 visitors per day**, was begun in **70 A.D.** by the **emperor Vespasian**. It was finished and inaugurated by his son and successor, **Titus** in **80 A.D.** What an amazing accomplishment it was to build such a structure in the first century A.D. in ten short years! The family name of the two emperors was Flavius, so the official name of the amphitheater was the **Flavian Amphitheater**. Only in the Middle Ages did it get the name **Colosseum**, probably from the **colossal statue of Nero** which stood next to it.

A curiosity

• There is an interesting **legend** which offers a different explanation for the name Colosseum. The building was said to have become a center of **satanic rites**, and the witches would ask in Latin the following question of their disciples: *Colis eum?* (Do you worship him?, referring to the devil). Combining the two Latin words, you get **Coliseum**.

The amphitheater was the scene of **brutal gladiatorial fights** which continued through the middle of the fifth century. There were also **wild beast fights** which went on for another hundred years after that. When it ceased to be used for these purposes in the Middle Ages it was taken over by some of Rome's aristocratic families and converted into their family fortress. By the **fifteenth century** it had become a **public stone quarry** and many of the city's renaissance palaces and even churches were built with stone taken from the Colosseum. The looting of materials stopped in the 1700's when the popes began to take an interest in preserving it. The building was never faced with marble, as some people think; it was built of stone, and the outside wall we see today is the same wall which the Romans saw.

A curiosity

• The amphitheater was built on the spot where it now stands for a particular reason. This area of Rome was part of the compound which contained the famous **Golden House of Nero**. On the very spot where the Colosseum is now there used to be an **artificial lake**, created by Nero for his personal enjoyment. After his death, his successor, Vespasian, wanted to do something special for the people who had been so brutally mistreated by Nero, so he had the lake drained and the Colosseum built for the enjoyment of the public. An excellent **public relations** move on his part!

The Romans built many amphitheaters all over the Roman Empire, but this was the largest and most elaborate of all. It is estimated that the seating capacity was about **50,000**. The spectators entered by means of one of **eighty arches** around the ground floor. The arches on the upper floors were decorated with **colossal statues of athletes**. You can still see today, above the ground-floor arches, the **Roman numerals** which would have corresponded to a number on your ticket, a practice very much like our system of entering stadiums today. The big difference between then and now is that the tickets were distributed to the Romans **free of charge**!

A curiosity

• There is one gate between entrances XXXVIII and XXXIX which has no number on it. This was an entrance reserved for the **emperor** and his guests.

As was the case with Roman theaters, the Colosseum could be covered with a **canvas awning** to protect the spectators from inclement weather. (And we thought WE had invented the domed stadium!) **Sailors** were in charge of operating the intricate canvas rigging. Around the top of the structure today, you can see protruding bases with holes in them. These were used to support the poles which held the canvas awnings

The interior of the Colosseum seen from the upper level.

A curiosity

- The floor was made of wood, covered by a **layer of sand** to keep the combatants from slipping and **to absorb the blood**. The Latin word for "sand" is (h)arena, and that is why to this day we sometimes use the word "arena" to refer to an athletic stadium.

There was also a **five-meter high wall** around the floor to protect the spectators from the action. The wall also allowed for the **flooding of the floor** and the presentation of **naval battles**.

When the popes began protecting the Colosseum in the eighteenth century, they did so partly because of the belief that many Christians had been martyred there. While it is true that many prisoners were executed in the Colosseum, we have **no historical evidence** to support the belief that people were put to death in this place simply **because they were Christians**. Nevertheless, the tradition of treating the Colosseum as a **holy place** continues today. Every year on **Good Friday** the pope leads a **Way of the Cross** ceremony at the amphitheater, which is telecast live all over the world.

The Colosseum rises up beyond the Roman Forum

Whenever there is an **earthquake** which is felt even slightly in Rome, the Colosseum is always one of the first buildings checked for damages after the quake. Fortunately there has not been any earthquake damage to the Colosseum in modern times, although it has been severely damaged by earthquakes several times in its almost two thousand year history. But perhaps the authorities are quick to check for damage because of the famous quotation of the **Venerable Bede** back in the **eighth century**:

Quamdiu stat Colisaeus, stat et Roma; quando cadet Colisaeus, cadet et Roma; quando cadet Roma, cadet et mundus.

(As long as the Colosseum stands, Rome also stands; when the Colosseum will fall, Rome will also fall; when Rome will fall, the world will also fall.)

Palazzo Massimo alle Terme. Who knows if the boxer didn't fight in the Colosseum?

The Column of the Immaculate Conception near the Spanish Steps.

Chapter 6

The Column of the Immaculate Conception
A December tradition

King David, one of the statues on the base
of the column.

Every year on **December 8**, Italy celebrates the feast of the **Immaculate Conception**, which is one of this country's most traditional and popular national holidays, recognized both as a religious feast day and secular holiday. The Italians call it simply *l'Immacolata*. It's one of several examples of that uniquely Italian mixture of the secular and the religious. The highlight of this feast is the **visit of the pope** to the *Colonna dell'Immacolata* (Column of the Immaculate Conception), a column which stands just a few yards away from the famous **Spanish Steps**.

The presence of the pope in the piazza on this day is an unbroken tradition since it was begun by **Pope Pius XII** in **1956**. The column itself is actually an **ancient Roman column** which was discovered on the grounds of a monastery in Rome in **1778** and which now has at its top a **bronze statue of the Virgin Mary**. The ancient column was only 12 meters high, so it was decided to place it atop an enormous base so that it would not be over-shadowed by the surrounding buildings.

The column and statue were set up by **Pius IX (1846-1878)** to recall his proclamation on **December 8, 1854**, of the dogma which declares Mary, the Mother of God, to be the only human being conceived **without original sin**. This concept had been believed for centuries by the faithful, but it only became official with the declaration of the dogma.

A curiosity

• The column was placed on this spot, almost directly in front of the **Spanish Embassy to the Vatican** because Spain was the country which had done the most to promote the proclamation of the dogma. The official dedication of the column took place on **December 8, 1856**, even though the statue of the Virgin was not ready yet and would not be in place at the top of the column until a few months later.

The huge base of the column is decorated with large statues representing the Old Testament figures of **Moses, David, Isaiah** and **Ezekiel**, and panels illustrating the **Annunciation**, the **Dream of St. Joseph**, the **Coronation of the Virgin** and the **Proclamation of the Dogma**. It is, indeed, a very impressive monument.

An interesting and very popular tradition was begun on **December 8, 1929**, when the **firemen of Rome** first placed a wreath at the column, asking the

Madonna for her protection in their dangerous work. The idea caught on and soon other organizations began to do the same thing, so that now, in addition to the firemen, just about every association and organization imaginable brings a **floral offering** to place at the foot of the column. You'll see representatives of the police, street cleaners, lawyers, doctors, electricians, plumbers, pharmacists, teachers, students, waiters, businessmen, church parishes and many others present their offering at various times during the day. By evening the column is literally surrounded by a colorful array of flowers.

A curiosity

• Since the firemen started the tradition, they have the honor of being the **first group** to present their offering early in the morning of the feast day, and they do it in a way which is unique to their profession. Using one of their **fire ladders**, a fire-fighter climbs to the top of the column and lays a wreath on the outstretched arm of the statue, where it will remain until the following year's celebration.

The climax of the day, about 4:00 in the afternoon, is the **arrival of the pope**, who travels in a slow-moving motorcade from the Vatican to Piazza di Spagna. Waiting at the column to welcome the pontiff is an array of ecclesiastical and secular officials, headed by the **Mayor of Rome** and the **Cardinal Vicar** who administers the Diocese of Rome on behalf of the pope.

The floral offering of the pontiff is traditionally the most impressive of all: a wreath of **300 roses** prepared by **Vatican gardeners**. In the late evening the papal wreath is transferred to the nearby church of **Sant'Andrea delle Fratte** and placed in front of a statue of the Madonna. Some of the other large floral pieces are also moved into various churches. Then the following morning, the flowers which are still in good shape are distributed to numerous chapels and religious institutes in the city.

The Spanish Embassy to the Vatican. The column was placed in front of it to thank Spain for its support for the dogma.

Michelangelo's dome looms above St. Peter's Basilica.
(Photo by Gianfranco Mandas)

Chapter 7

The Dome of St. Peter's Basilica
Behind the scenes

The dome seen from the Vatican Gardens
behind the basilica.

Michelangelo became chief architect of St. Peter's Basilica in **1546 at the age of seventy-two**. He remained in that job for the next eighteen years until his death in **1564 at the age of eighty-nine**. Over his long lifetime, Michelangelo completed many famous masterpieces, such as the frescoes in the Sistine Chapel, the David, the Moses, the Pietà and many others. However, he also left many works unfinished, which had to be completed by others after his death. The most famous of the works he did not live to see completed and the one which is the largest and certainly the most visible, is the **dome of St. Peter's Basilica**, known to the Romans as *il cupolone*. There are many domes in the Eternal City, but when you say *il cupolone*, there will be no question about what dome you are talking about.

The dome was not raised in Michelangelo's lifetime. At the time of his death it existed only on paper and in the form of a fifteen-foot model which he had built. For twenty-one years after his death no serious attempt was made to raise the dome according to his specifications. Perhaps his successors were intimidated by his bold design and didn't feel competent to realize it. What-

The dome seen from the Janiculum hill.

ever the reason, the dome remained unfinished until, in **1585, Felice Peretti** was elected pope, taking the name **Sixtus V**.

Sixtus was not in good health and he knew he would not have a long pontificate. He was determined, however, to see the dome of St. Peter's raised in his lifetime. He summoned his two architects, **Giacomo Della Porta** and **Domenico Fontana**, and instructed them to prepare a plan for completing Michelangelo's dome and to present it to him for his approval. Della Porta, who had worked under Michelangelo in his youth, had already finished other works of his mentor, such as **Palazzo Farnese** and the **Campidoglio**, always being careful to follow the design of the master. But the plan for raising the dome which he and Fontana presented to Sixtus in the **summer of 1588** was quite different from Michelangelo's plan.

A curiosity

• The presentation of the plan to the pope took place on the immense open floor of the **Basilica of St. Paul Outside the Walls** where the architects had room to spread out their design. Della Porta and Fontana presented their draft and nervously awaited the reaction of Sixtus who had been listening in rapt silence. At the end of the presentation, the pontiff asked only one question: "How long will it take?" The architects were taken aback by the question and didn't know what to answer. They knew that Brunelleschi's dome in Florence had taken **sixteen years** to raise. So Della Porta boldly gave what he considered a very optimistic estimate: "Ten years", he said to the pope. Sixtus shot back: "I'll give you thirty months." The architects were staggered by the pope's demand, but when Sixtus promised all the money, workmen and materials necessary to do the job, they accepted the challenge.

Work began immediately and continued non-stop in two twelve-hour shifts, twenty-four hours a day, seven days a week. The workmen paused only for one hour on Sundays while Mass was celebrated in the basilica. The result? The dome was raised in an incredible **twenty-two months**, eight fewer than the thirty which had been dictated by the pope! The

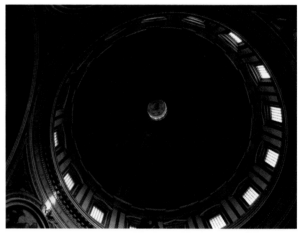

Looking up at the interior of the great dome.

final stone, stamped with the name of Sixtus V, was laid on **May 14, 1590**. The pontiff died just three months later, on **August 27**. His wish to see the dome completed in his lifetime had been fulfilled.

So when we talk about "Michelangelo's dome", we should at least add a little footnote giving credit for its completion to Giacomo Della Porta and Domenico Fontana, and yes, even to Sixtus V who pushed them so hard!

The façade of Santa Maria in Trastevere seen through the fountain.
(Photo by Gianfranco Mandas)

Chapter 8

Fons Olei
Origins of a great basilica

The façade and bell tower of
Santa Maria in Trastevere.

There is a tiny street in the picturesque neighborhood of **Trastevere**, just off Piazza Santa Maria in Trastevere, which has the odd name of *Via della Fonte d'Olio* (Fountain of Oil Street). It owes this unusual name to a **two-thousand year old legendary story** which also explains the origin of the **Basilica of Santa Maria in Trastevere**, one of the most beautiful and oldest churches in Rome.

According to the legend, on this site in **ancient Rome** there was an **inn for retired Roman soldiers**, called in Latin *taberna meritoria*. In the year **38 B.C.** there appeared a mysterious flow of an **oily liquid** on the site of the inn. The Jews, who inhabited this area at the time, considered this a **miraculous event** which foretold the imminent coming of the **Messiah**. Shortly after this, **Jesus Christ** was born, but he was not accepted by the Jewish people as their Messiah. Later, the early **Christians** looked back at this legend and said that the flow of oil must have been a sign of the **coming of Christ**.

A curiosity

• It's interesting to see the reasoning behind the Christians' interpretation of this event. The name **Christ** means **the anointed one**, and since anointing is done with oil, the miraculous flow of oil shortly before the coming of Christ must have signified his imminent birth.

From that time the site of the taberna meritoria was considered sacred by the Christians. **Pope Calixtus I (217-222)**, recognizing the importance of the site to the faithful, built a **small shrine** on the spot, which he called *Fons Olei* (fountain of oil), dedicating it to the **Mother of God**. It was over this shrine that **Julius I (337-352)** built the first real basilica with the name **Santa Maria**.

A curiosity

• It is believed that this was the **first church** in Rome to be dedicated to the Virgin Mary. As other churches were built and also dedicated to the Madonna, something had to be added to the names to distinguish them from each other. So this church became Santa Maria **in Trastevere**, to set it apart from Santa Maria **Maggiore**, or Santa Maria **della Vittoria** and the scores of other churches in Rome with the name of Santa Maria.

The basilica built by Julius in the fourth century was restored many times until the time of **Pope Innocent II (1130-1143)**, a native of the Trastevere neighborhood. He decided to **completely rebuild** the church which by that time was in a serious state of disrepair. The basilica which we see and admire today is substantially the reconstructed church from the **twelfth century**.

Inside the basilica is a beautiful **Latin inscription** on the ceiling of the main aisle near the altar. Few people notice it and fewer still try to read it, but it's important because it refers to the **traditional origins** of the basilica.

IN HAC PRIMA DEI MATRIS AEDE
TABERNA OLIM MERITORIA
OLEI FONS E SOLO ERUMPENS
CHRISTI ORTUM PORTENDIT

(In this first temple of the Mother of God, once a *taberna meritoria*, a fountain of oil, bursting out from the ground, predicted the birth of Christ).

Fons Olei: The spot where tradition says the oil flowed in the first century B.C.

Other curiosities

• On the right side of the church, near the sanctuary, is a marker with the Latin words *Fons Olei* (fountain of oil). It marks the spot of the legendary oil flow in 38 B.C.

• One of the magnificent **thirteenth-century mosaics** in the apse of the church depicting the **Nativity scene** includes a small building, beneath which are the words *taberna meritoria*, recalling the legendary beginnings of the church.

• The two side aisles are separated from the main aisle by **ancient Roman columns**, many of which were taken from the third-century **Baths of Caracalla**.

• In the **Altemps Chapel** at the end of the left aisle is the oldest Christian decoration in the church, a much prized **canvas painting** of the Virgin and Child, which has been dated to the sixth or seventh century.

• The walls of the **atrium** of the church are decorated in a very unusual way with **marble funeral markers**, both Christian and pagan, some of which come from the **catacombs**.

• In the sanctuary is a magnificent **thirteenth-century marble Paschal candelabrum** in the shape of a **twisting column** with mosaic decorations.

• The last figure on the left of the mosaic in the apse represents **Innocent II** who rebuilt the church in the twelfth century. The pontiff is holding in his hands a **model of the church**, as if he were presenting it to Mary and Jesus who are shown in the center of the same mosaic. Notice that Jesus, in a very human gesture, has his arm around his mother's shoulder.

There are many other beautiful paintings, mosaics and monuments in the basilica, but perhaps the best thing of all is the **sense of peace and tranquility** that people inevitably feel as they sit or walk around in the church, while soft organ music or Gregorian chant plays in the background.

And one final note: I'm proud to call Santa Maria in Trastevere **my parish church**!

The main altar of the basilica. (Photo by Gianfranco Mandas)

The replacement statue of the javelin thrower in the Stadium of the Marble Statues.

Chapter 9

Foro Italico
The modern Roman Forum

Mussolini Dux: The obelisk in front of the
Olympic Stadium.

Every person who visits Rome knows about the ancient **Roman Forum** in the center of the city. But just to the north of the Vatican, along the Tiber River is an enormous sports complex which could be considered the modern Roman Forum. Most of the complex was built between **1927** and **1933** during the fascist era at what was probably the height of the power and popularity of **Benito Mussolini**, *il Duce*. The area was originally named **Foro Mussolini**, but that name was changed after World War II to the name it holds today, **Foro Italico**. The complex was one of the great urban architectural successes of the fascist regime. The intention was to glorify athletic activity and at the same time unite it with **fascist ideology**.

In the piazza in front of the complex is the **Mussolini Obelisk**. Set up in **1932**, it stands over 36 meters high, including the base. It was made out of **white Carrara marble** and is one of the few monuments in Rome which still has the Mussolini name prominently displayed. In huge letters down the length of the obelisk we see written in Latin: *Mussolini Dux*. It would be difficult to remove or change the letters without defacing the obelisk.

The Foro Italico is also home to both indoor and outdoor swimming pools. The walls and floor of the pool building are covered with **mosaics**. Tennis courts are also part of the scene, but the largest structure in the complex is the **Stadio Olimpico**, the Olympic Stadium. It was built in the 1950's in preparation for the **1960 Rome Olympic Games** and now serves as the home field for Rome's two major league soccer teams, **Roma** and **Lazio**. The stadium, which can seat about 80,000 people, underwent major restoration in 1990 in preparation for the **World Cup Soccer** matches which Italy hosted that year.

But the most interesting and beautiful structure in the entire complex is the **Stadio dei marmi** (Stadium of the marble statues). Built between **1928** and **1935**, it has a seating capacity of 20,000. All around the top of the stadium, above the seating area, are sixty enormous **marble statues** of athletes.

A curiosity

• In the 1960's, one of these statues, the **javelin thrower**, was destroyed when hit by lightning, leaving fifty-nine statues and one empty space. The situation remained that way for **forty years** until, in 2006, an exact copy of the original javelin thrower was made out of magnificent Carrara marble. In a big public ceremony it was returned to its place in the stadium, thus completing once again the full circle of sixty statues.

The base of each statue bears the name of one of Italy's **provincial capital cities**. The stadium is still used today, often for special exhibition games. Such was the case a few years ago when, as a show of solidarity after the 9/11 disaster, the stadium hosted a special benefit soccer match between members of the **fire departments** of Rome and New York City. More recently, this unique stadium was used as the stage for the opening ceremonies of the **World Swimming Championships** in July, 2009, which the city of Rome hosted.

If you want an unusual and interesting means of transportation to the Foro Italico, you can take the **tour boat** up the Tiber. To enjoy the entire route of the boat ride, you should board at the starting point just below Ponte Garibaldi at the **Tiber Island**. When you get off at the last stop you'll find yourself face-to-face with the Mussolini Obelisk and the Olympic Stadium.

A partial view of the Stadium of the Marble Statues.

The only surviving ancient statue of Julius Caesar is in Rome's City Council Chambers.

Chapter 10

Gregory vs. Caesar
A papal "eclipse"

The bronze statue of Julius Caesar near
his forum.

Among the many extraordinary monuments in **St. Peter's Basilica** there is one which appeals to me in a special way because of its **historic signifi-cance**. In the right side aisle of the basilica, just beyond the Chapel of the Most Holy Sacrament, is the white marble monument of **Gregory XIII Boncompagni (1572-1585)**.

The monument is a handsome one, depicting the pontiff seated, his right hand raised in blessing. High above the statue of the pope is the Boncompagni family **coat of arms** featuring the **dragon** which appears again in a carving at the bottom of the monument. Below the figure of the pope is a **sarcophagus** flanked by two allegorical female figures representing the virtues of **Faith** (to the left) and **Wisdom**. The statue representing Wisdom is shown **uncovering the sarcophagus** to reveal a carving which recalls the **most important event** in Gregory's papacy, an event which remains timely over 400 years later: the **reform of the calendar**.

A curiosity

• The statue of Wisdom on the monument is represented with a military **helmet and shield**, which at first might seem a bit inappropriate for the scene. The artist, however, is depicting Wisdom in the guise of **Minerva**, the Roman goddess of wisdom and war, a representation which is not at all unusual in Christian art.

Gregory XIII was a very learned man who nourished a great passion for **astronomy**. He utilized the **Tower of the Winds** inside the Vatican, turning it into an observatory/laboratory for his astronomers. This eventually evolved into the prestigious **Vatican Observatory**, which has since been moved to the summer papal residence in **Castel Gandolfo** just to the south of Rome.

In the sixteenth century most of the world was still using the **Julian calendar** which had been introduced by **Julius Caesar** in **46 B.C.** In **1582**, after much study and many calculations, Gregory's astronomers informed him that the Julian calendar, which had been in use for over **1,600 years**, was **ten days off** in respect to solar time. The carving on the sarcophagus which is being unveiled by the figure of Wisdom shows the pope seated on a throne with one hand resting on a globe, while his astronomers explain their calculations to him.

A curiosity

• So how did Gregory solve the problem of the ten-day discrepancy? Simple. He just **cancelled ten days** from the year! People went to bed on the night of **October 4, 1582**, and when they woke up the next morning it was **October 15**, by papal decree! The ten days from October 5 through October 14 simply **did not exist** that year.

Apart from the scientific importance of this event, there was also a very strong **symbolic importance** which certainly did not go unnoticed. It was the **pope** correcting the **dictator**; it was the **Roman papacy** surpassing the **Roman empire**.

At first the change was accepted only by the **Catholic rulers** in Europe, but gradually this new calendar was also adopted by Protestant countries, including **Great Britain in 1700**. And in the twentieth century the new calendar was even adopted by **Communist China** and the **Soviet Union**. This calendar, still in use today after over 400 years, carries the name of its papal creator: the **Gregorian calendar**.

A partial view of the monument of Gregory XIII
in St. Peter's Basilica. (Photo by Gianfranco Mandas)

The base of the monument to Giuseppe Garibaldi on the Janiculum hill.

Chapter 11

The Janiculum Hill
Heroes and martyrs

Garibaldi keeps watch over the city from
the top of the Janiculum.

The year **1849** was one of the most crucial and dramatic years of the Italian *Risorgimento*. For years the popular movement for a united, free and independent Italy had been growing. **Pius IX (1846-1878)** had been forced to flee the city to **Gaeta**, a small town on the coast a few miles southwest of Rome. This brought about the **collapse of the Papal States**, and a **Republic** was declared on **February 9, 1849**, led by a triumvirate headed by **Giuseppe Mazzini**.

Pius IX, however, in exile at Gaeta, appealed to the Catholic nations of France, Austria, Spain and the Kingdom of the Two Sicilies for help against the insurgents. The **French** in particular responded by sending a force of **10,000 men** led by **General Oudinot**, which landed at the port of **Civitavecchia**, just northwest of Rome, on **April 24**.

The Italian patriots, led by **Giuseppe Garibaldi**, prepared to defend their newly established Republic, making their stand on the **Janiculum**. Against the 10,000 French troops, Garibaldi could muster only **7,000 men**, and they were poorly armed at that. Oudinot's troops attacked on **April 30** at the **Porta San Pancrazio**, one of the gates leading into the city through the papal walls.

A curiosity

• The French, because of their numerical superiority, expected little resistance from the Italians. However, not only was the defense much stronger than expected, but Garibaldi himself boldly led his bayoneted troops in a **counter attack** out from the San Pancrazio Gate, forcing the French to retreat.

The two sides agreed to a **truce**, during which the French troops received reinforcements, bringing their number to **37,000**. The Italians, too, were reinforced during the truce, and they now numbered **19,000**, still woefully few compared to the French forces. The days of the Republic were numbered! On **June 1**, Oudinot declared an **end to the truce**, anouncing that he would attack on **June 4**. Instead, he made a deceitful sneak-attack **during the night** between June 2 and 3, catching the defenders by surprise. Although the Italians fought courageously, they were soon overwhelmed by the massive numbers of the French troops.

The **final attack** came on **June 30** when the French finally broke through the walls at the San Pancrazio gate. On **July 4**, the Republic decided to end all resistance in order to avoid further bloodshed and destruction in the city. Garibaldi, along with his wife **Anita**, fled the city, heading for the safety of Venice. Anita, pregnant and seriously ill, **died on the journey**. She was **28 years old**.

Curiosities

• Among the famous casualties of the fighting was the twenty-one-year-old **Goffredo Mameli**, a poet whose composition *Fratelli d'Italia* became the **Italian National Anthem**. Though not a soldier, he had decided to fight for the unification of his country. Both he and Anita Garibaldi are buried on the Janiculum. Today the top of the hill is lined with **marble busts** of many of those who fought with Garibaldi in those historic battles of 1849. One of these busts is regularly washed and kept cleaner and whiter than the rest. The name on its base reads: GOFFREDO MAMELI.

Bust of Goffredo Mameli, author of the Italian National Anthem.

• The church of **San Pietro in Montorio** stands on the Janiculum just down the street from the Porta San Pancrazio which was one of the main targets of the French forces. Although this **fifteenth-century** church was not itself a target, it nevertheless was in the line of fire and sustained heavy damage, particularly from the **French cannon fire**. The damage, of course, has long since been repaired, but in the **1990's** while some modern repair work was being done in the church, workers made an **astounding discovery**. They found, embedded inside a wall which they were working on, a **French cannon ball** which had hit the church over **140 years before**! It was taken out and attached to a plaque which can now be seen on the outside wall of the church. A vivid reminder of the fierce fighting which took place here in 1849.

Capitoline Museums: Bust of Michelangelo. (Photo by Gianfranco Mandas)

Chapter 12

Laocoon
Timeo Danaos . . . I fear the Greeks . . .

Vatican Museums: Laocoon and his two
sons are attacked by the serpents.

The modern entrance to the **Vatican Museums** was built for the **Jubilee Year of 2000**. To the right of this modern entrance is a large portal built into the sixteenth-century walls. Before the year 2000, this portal served as both entrance and exit of the museums. Today the new opening is the entrance and the old portal is the exit.

A curiosity

• Look up at the exit portal and you will see **two statues** which very few people seem to notice. They portray two of the most famous artists whose works are in the museum. On the left is **Michelangelo**, sculptor, depicted holding a **chisel** and **mallet**, the tools of his trade. On the right is **Raphael**, painter, depicted with **palette** and **paintbrushes**, the tools of his trade. Notice that Michelangelo is represented as an **older man** (he died at age 89), and Raphael is shown as a much younger man (he died at age 38). In between the two statues is the coat of arms of **Pius XI (1922-1939)** who opened this portal in **1932**. Remember, this portal is now the exit, but was originally the entrance, so it is as if Michelangelo and Raphael were positioned above the entrance to welcome the visitors into the museum.

If I had to pick my favorite area among the seemingly endless rooms and hallways which are the Vatican Museums, I would choose the **Octagonal Courtyard of the Belvedere**, built on a design by **Bramante**. When **Giuliano Della Rovere** was elected **Pope Julius II in 1503**, he began to furnish the courtyard with some pieces from his extensive private collection of ancient sculptures. He then invited the artists of the day to come and view and even sketch these great works of art. This was really the beginning of the Vatican Museums. Among the works of art in the courtyard are four statues which have a particular importance: **Apollo, Laocoon, Hermes** and **Perseus**. Of these four, my personal favorite is the Laocoon. In order to really appreciate the statue, you must know the story of the episode which it represents. You can read a vivid description of this entire episode in **Vergil's *Aeneid*** (Book II, lines 199-233). What follows here is the story in a nutshell.

Nero. Laocoon was found in his Golden House.

The drama is set near the end of the ten-year war between the **Trojans** and the **Greeks**. The war appeared to end with the victory of the Trojans, as the Greeks apparently abandoned the battlefields and sailed away (only to hide behind a nearby island). The Trojans poured out of the walled city to celebrate and they discovered a strange "gift" left behind by the Greeks: an enormous **wooden horse**. They were planning to bring it into the city as a spoil of war, but there was a dissenting voice in the crowd. It was **Laocoon, priest of Apollo**, who warned the Trojans not to bring the horse into the city. His famous warning, as related by Vergil, goes like this:

. . . equo ne credite, Teucri.
Quidquid id est, timeo Danaos et dona ferentes.

(Do not trust the horse, Trojans. Whatever it is, I fear the Greeks even bearing gifts.) [*Aeneid, 2, 48-49*].

Despite this ominous warning, the Trojans brought the horse into the city. That night a small band of Greeks, hidden in the **belly of the horse**, silently slipped out and opened the gates for the rest of the Greeks who then entered the city and slaughtered the Trojans.

The goddess **Minerva**, who had sided with the Greeks during the war, decided to punish Laocoon for trying to help the Trojans. She sent **two serpents** from the sea to kill him and his two sons. This attack by the serpents is the subject of the statue group. It graphically depicts Laocoon and his sons struggling to free themselves from the coils of the serpents.

Minerva sent the serpents.

A curiosity

• The statue of Laocoon was discovered in **1506** in the **Domus Aurea** (Golden House) of **Nero** near the Colosseum. It was immediately identified as the **ancient Greek marble statue** which had been described by **Pliny the Elder** in the **first century A.D.** The moment Julius II learned of the discovery, he sent Michelangelo himself to supervise the recovery of the statue and its transfer to the Belvedere courtyard. The statue, with its **twisting figures**, had a profound effect on Michelangelo.

One of the most fascinating things about this sculpture group is the story about the **right arm** of Laocoon. When the statue was discovered in 1506 it was in relatively good condition, but missing its right arm. It was decided to have someone sculpt a right arm and attach it to the statue. Michelangelo himself began to sculpt a replacement-arm, but he never finished it. In the meantime, another sculptor, **Montorsoli**, was hired to create a new arm which he sculpted in a **stretched-out position**. Almost 400 years later, in **1905**, the **original arm** of the statue was found. It was in a **bent position**, depicting Laocoon as if he were trying to tear the serpents off his body. This was **totally different** from the Montorsoli re-creation. Only in **1960** was the Montorsoli arm removed and the original arm reattached.

Curiosities

• So what became of the arm which Michelangelo carved? Well, it still exists, and amazingly, his version of the arm is in a **bent position**, very similar to the original which was unknown until 1905. Michelangelo, with his knowledge of the human body and its muscular system, had understood what the original arm must have looked like!

• When the Montorsoli arm was removed in 1960, and before they reattached the original arm, they temporarily put the Michelangelo arm on the statue and saw that, despite the fact that it was un-finished, it was indeed **almost identical** to the original. In the **Vatican archives** is an amazing photograph of the statue with the Michelangelo arm attached.

Vatican Picture Gallery: Pope Julius II.

Michelangelo and Raphael look down from above the old entrance
(now the exit) to the Vatican Museums

Et tu, Brute! Caesar was assassinated just behind the round temple.

Chapter 13

Largo Argentina
Temples, cats and . . . !

A partial view of the temples in
Largo Argentina.

There is a curious place in the middle of Rome called *Area Sacra di Largo Argentina* (the Sacred Area of Largo Argentina), which is famous for more than one reason and which has a very interesting history behind it. The area was demolished between **1926–1929** in order to widen streets and further develop that part of the city. But as usually happens in this city, when they started digging in order to lay the foundations for modern buildings they began to uncover remains from **ancient Rome**. This time it was clear to the archaeologists that the Roman remains were substantial, so the development of the area was abandoned and an **archaeological site** was created.

A curiosity

• Various accounts have been put forth to explain the origin of the name *Largo Argentina*. "Largo" is another name for *piazza* (square), but it is the "Argentina" part of the name which is interesting. One thing is sure: the name has nothing to do with Argentina, the country. There is a **medieval tower** here which was built for an important bishop from Strasbourg. The Latin word for Strasbourg is *Argentoratus,* so the tower became known in Latin as the *Turris Argentorata* (Strasbourg Tower). *Argentina*, therefore, is simply a corruption of the word *argentorata* and eventually was applied not only to the tower, but to the square as well, hence *Largo Argentina*. The *Area Sacra* (sacred area) part of the full name comes, of course, from the discovery of the sacred temples in the middle of the square.

What the archaeologists discovered here was an ancient Roman **temple precinct** consisting of **four temples** from the Republican period lined up side by side. The temples were built at different times between the **forth and second centuries B.C.**, making them some of the oldest surviving Roman ruins in the city. There is no agreement among scholars about the deities to whom the temples were dedicated.

The most exciting information about this area is what happened right behind the little **round temple**. Here was the *Curia Pompei*, a large building with a steep flight of steps leading up to its entrance. This building was dedicated to **Pompey**, the arch-rival of **Julius Caesar**. The Roman Senate often held its sessions in buildings such as this around the city. In fact, the senate was planning to do just that on **March 15, 44 B.C.** Yes, it was the **Ides of March**, and as Caesar was climbing the steps to enter the Curia building **he was assassinated** by **Brutus** and **Cassius** and about twenty other senators. Caesar was reportedly fighting off his attackers, but when he saw that Brutus, his adopted son and chosen heir, was among them, he stopped struggling and exclaimed in disbelief: *Et tu Brute?* (You, too, Brutus?).

A curiosity

• After the assassination, Caesar's body was taken to the nearby **Roman Forum** where **Marc Antony** gave the famous funeral oration which whipped the crowd into such a frenzy that they prematurely set fire to the bier, cremating Caesar's body. Because the oration and cremation took place in the Forum, and because Caesar was killed while he was preparing to attend a meeting of the Senate, many people assume that he was killed in the Forum. But you must remember that the session of the Senate that day was to be held in the *Curia Pompei*, now Largo Argentina.

However, Caesar and the famous Republican temples are often upstaged by **the cats**! The area is home to over **two hundred stray cats** who receive tender loving care and lots of food from volunteer workers. There is a city ordinance in Rome which protects stray cats in the city, giving them the right to "take up residence" wherever they please without fear of being evicted. Many of the strays have chosen this spot because it is free of both automobile and pedestrian traffic, but there are many small colonies of strays all over Rome which are cared for by roving *gattare* (cat ladies).

Cats lounge in heavenly bliss in the safety of the ruins.

Palazzo Bonaparte with the famous balcony of Letizia, Napoleon's mother.

Chapter 14

A Mysterious Visitor
Who WAS that guy?

A close-up of
Letizia Bonaparte's balcony.

I had always wanted to know what that little green, covered balcony was – the one overlooking **Piazza Venezia** at its intersection with **Via del Corso** in the very center of Rome. I had asked long-time residents and natives of Rome about it, but nobody was able to explain the balcony to me. Well, I finally satisfied my curiosity thanks to an extraordinary two-day opening of this palazzo which is ordinarily closed to the public.

The present building was constructed between 1658 and 1667, but what makes it particularly interesting is that in 1818 it came into the possession of the **Bonaparte** family. And in fact, the name *Bonaparte* is clearly visible at the very top of the palazzo, but somehow I had never noticed it before. Also the Bonaparte family **coat of arms** can be seen above the middle window on the second floor. In addition to the beautiful frescoed walls and ceilings, the building houses a colossal **statue of Napoleon**, represented as **Mars**, the Roman god of war.

Letizia Bonaparte, the mother of Napoleon, spent the last twenty years of her life in retirement in this palazzo. She rarely went out and she would spend hours every day on her little balcony, observing the busy activity below in Piazza Venezia while remaining hidden from the prying eyes of the curious by the blinds of the balcony's covering. In fact, Donna Letizia died in the room just to the left of the balcony on **February 2, 1836**. The balcony itself has been left just as it was when she used it as her "observation post".

A curiosity

•   It usually surprises people to learn that Napoleon himself never set foot in Rome, despite the fact that in 1809 he annexed the city to his **French Empire**. In addition, when his son **Carlo Giuseppe Napoleon** was born in 1811, Napoleon had him proclaimed **King of Rome**.

Letizia received many visitors during her twenty years of residence in the palazzo, but one visit in particular is **cloaked in mystery**. Here is the story of that visit as told by Letizia's secretary. On the evening of **March 5, 1821**, an unknown man appeared at the palazzo saying it was urgent that he speak to Donna Letizia. When he was ushered into her presence, he said to her:

At this very moment at which I am speaking to you, His Majesty (Napoleon) is free from his pain and is happy. My Lady, kiss this crucifix, the Saviour of your son. You will see him again, but only after many years.

All later attempts to find this man were fruitless; he seemed to have vanished from the face of the earth. Who was the **mysterious visitor**? Nobody knows for sure, but consider the following interesting coincidencies:

- March 5, 1821, the date of the visit, is also the date of **Napoleon's death**.
- Letizia lived on for another **fifteen years** after the mysterious visit.
- Napoleon died in the **good graces of the Church** after a deathbed reconciliation.
- The mysterious visitor is said to have had the bearing and the voice of . . . **Napoleon himself!**

Now I never pass through Piazza Venezia without glancing up at Letizia's little covered balcony and thinking about her and her **mysterious visitor**.

The Bonaparte family coat of arms above the window on the façade of the building.

Fuoco! (Fire!) The cannon is fired every day at noon.

Chapter 15

The Noon Cannon Shot
You can set your watch!

When not in use the cannon is stored
behind this door beneath Piazzale Garibaldi.

Every day in Rome a **blank cannon shot** is fired from the **Janiculum hill** signaling 12:00 noon. This is a tradition very dear to residents and tourists alike. It goes back to **December 1, 1847**, when the first blast was fired from the roof of **Castel Sant'Angelo** on the banks of the Tiber River. The cannon remained in that location until **August 1, 1903**, when it was moved to **Monte Mario** which overlooks **St. Peter's Basilica** from the north. Then it was moved again on **January 24, 1924**, this time to the Janiculum hill, on a terrace just below **Piazzale Garibaldi**, where it remains to this day.

The tradition was interrupted in **1939** during **World War II** for obvious reasons, and when it resumed after the War, they substituted a **siren blast** for the cannon shot. This didn't sit well with the Romans, who insisted that the traditional cannon shot be restored. It took a while to convince the authorities, but finally, on **April 21, 1959**, as part of the celebration of the **birthday of Rome**, the cannon returned to action and has been firing ever since.

Curiosities

• So who actually fires the cannon every day at noon? Well, it all has to be done with **military precision** because this is an official signal of twelve noon, so the task of firing the cannon is entrusted to **three soldiers**. They arrive on the scene shortly before noon and wheel the cannon out from its storage space beneath the piazza to a platform on the terrace. There's a **countdown** in the military tradition and then . . . **Fuoco!** (Fire!). The locals know that the shot will be fired at exactly twelve noon, and you can see them checking their watches when they hear the blast.

• The explosive effect of the shot is obtained by a blank cartridge shell containing about two pounds of black gunpowder. It can be heard all over the city, but if you want to set your watch to the second, it will depend on where you are when you hear the shot. If you're on the Janiculum, you hear the shop at exactly 12:00, two seconds later in **Piazza Navona**, three seconds after noon if you're on **Montecitorio**, four from the **Quirinal hill**, five from **Piazza Barberini** and a full seven seconds after noon from **Termini** train station. If you're in a position down in the city from where you can see the Janiculum hill, look up in that direction and you'll see the **smoke** followed seconds later by the blast.

It's fun to watch the soldiers in action, so every day a small crowd gathers up on the hill to enjoy the spectacle. Try it the next time you're in Rome, but be sure to cover your ears if they are sensitive to loud noise!

A soldier awaits the order to fire the cannon.

Looking toward the oculus. (Photo by Gianfranco Mandas)

Chapter 16

The Pantheon
An imperial gift

The exterior of the Pantheon.

It was 1,400 years ago, **May 13, 609**, that **Pope Boniface IV (608-615)** consecrated the **Pantheon**, transforming it from a pagan temple dedicated to **all the gods**, into a Christian church dedicated to **Santa Maria ad Martyres** (St. Mary at the Martyrs). For the occasion the pontiff is said to have transferred to the church from the **catacombs** several cart-loads of **bones of Christian martyrs**.

A curiosity

• The Pantheon was a gift to the pope from the **Roman emperor Foca**. Shortly after the donation, the pontiff ordered that a column be erected in the **Roman Forum** in honor of the emperor, presumably to thank him for the donation. The **Column of Foca** still stands today. It was the last monument to be erected in the Forum.

The simple but beautiful **Latin inscription** across the façade of the building tells us who built it and when.

M. AGRIPPA L. F. COS. TERTIUM FECIT
(Marcus Agrippa, son of Lucius, consul for the third time, built it)

We know from our history that **Marcus Agrippa** was consul for the third time in the year **27 B.C.** Agrippa, besides holding the second highest office in the empire, was also the son-in-law and trusted adviser of the **emperor Augustus**.

The building we see today, however, is not the original Pantheon of Agrippa from 27 B.C. There were disastrous fires in this part of Rome both in the year 80 and in the year 110. Agrippa's Pantheon was so badly damaged in these fires that the **emperor Hadrian (117 – 138)** decided to tear it down and rebuild it. The new Pantheon was completed in **128** and that is the building we see today. It's interesting to note that Hadrian put Agrippa's inscription back up instead of putting his own name on it. An unusually humble act for a Roman emperor!

Over 1,400 years after its dedication as a church, the Pantheon continues to fulfill that role in our times. It remains an active church today, even though it is not an official parish church. Its transformation into a place of worship is, of course, what saved the building, making it today the **best preserved ancient monument in Rome**.

The Pantheon is the burial place of the great renaissance artist **Raphael (1483-1520)**. His very simple stone sarcophagus has an incredibly beautiful Latin inscription on it which was composed by **Cardinal Pietro Bembo:**

ILLE HIC EST RAPHAEL TIMUIT QUO SOSPITE VINCI RERUM
MAGNA PARENS ET MORIENTE MORI

(Here is that famous Raphael. When he was alive, the great Mother
of things [Nature] feared that she was being surpassed, and when
he was dying she feared that she herself was dying)

Not too shabby, having your works favorably compared to those of Mother Nature!

There are three other prominent tombs in the Pantheon. One holds the body of **Victor Emmanuel II**, the first king of a united Italy, buried here in 1878. Directly across from him is the tomb of his son and successor, **Umberto I**, assassinated in 1900. Just below Umberto's tomb is that of his wife, **Queen Margherita di Savoia** who died in 1926.

A curiosity

• Every time I see the tomb of Queen Margherita, I get an urge to go out for pizza. Here's why. In **1889,** the king and queen, Umberto and Margherita, were in **Naples** on vacation. Famed pizza maker **Rosa Brandi** and her husband **Raffaello Esposito** were called upon to supply the royal couple with some local culinary creation. For the occasion, Rosa and Raffaelo prepared a **patriotic pizza** with **tomato, mozzarella** and **basilico,** so as to have the three colors of the **Italian flag: red, white and green.** The pizza so pleased Queen Margherita that the pizza makers named it after her, hence the now famous and ever popular **Pizza Margherita.** The original **Pizzeria Brandi** is still in business today.

This amazing building is an architectural wonder which has been admired and studied for centuries by architects from around the world. **Michelangelo** analyzed its dome very carefully as he designed the great **cupola of St. Peter's Basilica.** At the top of the dome is the famous *oculus*, or eye, which measures nine meters across and which is the only source of light in the building. The *oculus* is never covered, either by glass to keep the rain out, or by netting to keep the birds out. So when it rains, the water comes in, but quickly drains out through a number of nearly invisible openings in the floor. And when birds get in, well, they just fly around inside until they find their way out again.

The Pantheon proper is preceded by a portico with **sixteen enormous monolithic columns of red or grey granite**. Originally the ceiling of this portico was covered with **bronze**, but in 1625 **Urban VIII Barberini (1623-1644)** ordered that the bronze be removed; he then instructed his architect **Bernini** to use it to build the **baldacchino**, or canopy, over the main altar of the newly completed St. Peter's Basilica. Bernini had some bronze left over so the pontiff had it turned into **cannonballs for Castel Sant'Angelo**! This pontifical stripping of the ceiling by the Barberini pope earned for him the satirical judgment:

Quod non fecerunt barbari, fecerunt Barberini
(What the barbarians did not do, the Barberini did)

Pentecost in the Pantheon

There is a beautiful tradition which is repeated every year in the Pantheon on **Pentecost Sunday**. Pentecost, from the Greek word meaning **fiftieth**, is a moveable feast in the Church. It occurs **fifty days after Easter** and celebrates the **descent of the Holy Spirit** on the Apostles in the form of **tongues of fire**. To commemorate this event, following a solemn Mass celebrated in the Pantheon, thousands of **red rose petals** are dropped down through the *oculus* at the top of the dome onto the congregation below. It's really an impressive sight as all those rose petals come drifting slowly down through the *oculus*.

This is an extremely old tradition, which began on Pentecost Sunday in the year **1303**. The Mass was celebrated that year by **Benedict XI (1303-1304)**. The custom continues to this day, although there have been periods when it was interrupted and then taken up again. Don't miss it if you're ever in Rome on a Pentecost Sunday.

A curiosity

•   The people who actually release the rose petals are some of Rome's *vigili del fuoco* (firemen), who climb along the outside of the dome to reach the oculus. Every year this reminds me of the time in the summer of **1972** when I was attending the summer program of the **American Academy in Rome**. The director that year was the late **Prof. John D'Arms** of the University of Michigan, and he arranged an activity for the summer schoolers that I will never forget. He obtained permission to lead us up the outside of the dome all the way up to the *oculus*, just like the firemen do on Pentecost Sunday. We were then able to lie down **flat on our stomachs** and actually peer down through the *oculus* into the Pantheon! It was an incredibly exhilarating and unforgettable adventure, one that very few people have ever had the opportunity to experience.

The Column of Foca in the Roman Forum. A thank-you gift
from a pope to an emperor.

The colossal statue of the Apostle in front of the Basilica of St. Paul Outside the Walls.

Chapter 17

Peter and Paul
Patron saints of Rome

The façade of the Basilica of
St. Paul Outside the Walls.

Every year on **June 29**, the city of Rome celebrates the feast of **Saints Peter and Paul**, a joint commemoration, the celebration of which goes back to the year **258**. Rome has always claimed a special relationship with these two saints, and their feast day on June 29 is an **official city holiday**. Both Peter and Paul lived in Rome and were imprisoned and martyred here, Peter by **crucifixion**, Paul by **beheading**.

A curiosity

• Peter was crucified **upside down** at his own request, telling his executioners he was not worthy to die in the same way as his Master. But why was Paul beheaded instead of crucified? After all, crucifixion was the usual manner of execution at that time. Paul was a **Roman citizen**, and therefore **exempt from crucifixion** which was considered the most ignoble method of execution, and as such, reserved for **non-Roman citizens**. Beheading was considered a more "humane" execution.

In the year **258** during the persecution under the **emperor Valerian**, the bodies of Peter and Paul were removed from their tombs and transferred to the **Catacombs of St. Sebastian** on the Appian Way because of fear that their tombs and bodies would be desecrated by the Romans. Almost a hundred years later, after the end of the persecutions, **Pope Sylvester I (314-335)** ordered that their bodies be returned to their original graves, but he kept their heads separated from their bodies. The heads were eventually placed in reliquaries above the main altar of the **Basilica of St. John Lateran** where they remain to this day.

The feast of Saints Peter and Paul is also the day on which the pope presents the *pallium* to newly named **archbishops** from around the world. The *pallium* is a narrow strip of white wool marked by small black crosses. It represents the **authority** invested in the archbishop who receives it. These *pallia* are kept throughout the year in an urn beneath the main altar of **St. Peter's Basilica**, directly above the **tomb of St. Peter**. Then on the feast day of Peter and Paul they are presented in a solemn ceremony to those who have been named archbishop during the preceding twelve months.

I wanted to include in this section some monument, church, painting, etc. which deals with both Peter and Paul together. I chose the **main doors of St. Peter's Basilica**, the decorations on which depict the two saints, including a graphic representation of their martyrdom.

The Doors of Filarete

Directly in front of you as you enter the atrium of St. Peter's Basilica are the magnificent **bronze central doors** leading into the basilica proper. These doors are one of the few items which have survived intact from the original basilica. They were completed by **Filarete in 1445**, so they were relatively new to the old basilica which was torn down beginning in **1506** by **Bramante**. This is a large **double door**, both parts of which contain two **rectangular panels** and one **square panel**. Each panel is enclosed by a frame and surrounded by a band decorated with leaves, animals, portraits and scenes of various types, some of which are taken from the stories of **pagan myths**.

The main decorations of the doors are what we see in the six panels. Of the two top panels, one depicts **Christ**, identified as *Salvator Mundi* (Saviour of the world), while the other one represents the **Virgin Mary** (*Ave Maria*). Both figures are shown seated on a throne. The two middle panels show **St. Paul** on the left and **St. Peter** on the right. The smaller figure kneeling at the feet of Peter and **receiving the keys** from him is **Pope Eugene IV (1431-1447)** who commissioned the door to Filarete. It was common for artists to represent in their work the person who commissioned it.

A curiosity

•   It's very easy to recognize representations of Peter and Paul by the attributes ascribed to them. Peter is almost always shown holding **keys** in his hand, recalling the proclamation of Christ: *I will give to you the keys of the Kingdom of Heaven.* Paul is usually portrayed with a **sword** because he was a persecutor of the Christians before his conversion, and because of the military-like zeal he showed in spreading the Faith after his conversion.

The two smaller, square panels at the bottom of the door are filled with interesting detail about the **martyrdom** of the two saints. The panel on the right is dedicated to Peter. On the upper right side of it, you see the **emperor Nero**, during whose persecution Peter was martyred. He is shown giving the order to a soldier to carry out the execution. You see Peter being led away, hands tied behind his back. Then you see him again at the top of the panel as he is being crucified upside down.

The lower panel on the left shows the emperor again, as he gives the order for the execution of Paul. Then we see Paul being led away, while the execution itself, by beheading, is shown at the bottom right. Notice that Paul appears to be **blindfolded** as he kneels awaiting the blow of the executioner. The story is told that a young girl who was witness to the execution **covered Paul's eyes** with her shawl. So at the top of the panel Filarete represents Paul a third time as he comes down from Heaven and **returns the shawl** to the girl.

In both of the panels representing the martyrdoms of the two apostles, Filarete wanted to accurately depict the scene in which they happened. In the martyrdom of Peter, you see at the bottom of the panel the **Tiber River** which flows nearby. There are also two **pyramid-shaped funeral monuments** which existed in this area, and finally, the **circular building** represents the nearby **Tomb of Hadrian**, known today as **Castel Sant'Angelo**. Of course these structures were not there at the time of Peter's martyrdom, but they were there in the mid fifteenth century when Filarete made the doors. The scene of Paul's martyrdom is decorated with **vegetation** and **birds** in flight because the execution took place on the *Via Ostiensis* outside the walls of the city in what was at the time a **rural setting**.

A curiosity

• When you go into the basilica, look at the inside of this door and you will see that Filarete **signed his work** in a unique and humorous manner. At the bottom of the door, in very small dimensions, he depicted himself **riding a donkey** into the city, led by a group of his celebrating students. He must have had a good sense of humor to sign such an important commission in this unusual and amusing way!

The doors of Filarete: A close-up of the panel which depicts the martydom of St. Peter.

The doors of Filarete in St. Peter's Basilica with their decorations
dealing with Peter and Paul.

The *Tempietto* of Bramante had the same effect on Julius II as did the *Pietà* of Michelangelo.

Chapter 18

The Pietà of Michelangelo
Beauty beyond description

The *Pietà* behind bullet-proof glass
in St. Peter's Basilica.

The *Pietà* was carved out of a **single block of Carrara marble**. The commission to carve the statue was given to **Michelangelo Buonarotti** by a French cardinal who wanted it for the Chapel of the King of France in the old St. Peter's Basilica. At the time of the commission, Michelangelo was only **twenty-three years old**, a totally unknown and unproven artist outside the small circle of artists in Florence under the patronage of the **Medici family**.

The story behind the commissioning of the sculpture tells us something about the faith that at least one person had in the skills of the young Florentine sculptor. That person was **Jacobo Galli**, a Roman banker who became a close friend and adviser to Michelangelo. It was Galli who made what must have been considered at the time a **rash promise** in the contract he drew up for the cardinal and the artist. In it he writes:

I, Jacobo Galli, promise to the most reverend cardinal that Michelangelo will create the aforesaid work of art within one year and that it will be the most beautiful work of marble which exists today in Rome, and that no other master could make it better.

Talk about going out on a limb for someone! Well, it took two years instead of one to complete, but the second part of the promise turned out to be a huge understatement!

A curiosity

• Shortly after the statue was completed and placed, unsigned, in the basilica, Michelangelo would often mingle unnoticed in the crowds in front of the sculpture, listening to the comments being made about it. One day he heard two men discussing who the mystery sculptor might be. One of them remarked: *This looks like the work of Cristoforo Solari of Milan.* This angered the young Michelangelo so much that he decided to make sure that no one would ever make that mistake again. He hid in the basilica that night and after he was left alone and locked inside, he went to work. Along the ribbon that stretches across the chest of Mary he sculpted in Latin: *Michael. Angelus. Bonarotus. Florent. Faciebat* (Michelangelo Buonarotti, a Florentine, made this). Later he regretted signing it, considering the act as something akin to a sin of pride. He would never again feel the need to sign any of his works.

If you look closely at the **face of Mary**, you will see that Michelangelo represented her as a **very young woman**, much too young to be the mother of the thirty-three year old Jesus. One explanation offered for this youthful appearance is the fact that the artist's own mother died when he was only six years old. Michelangelo sculpted the face of the Virgin Mary, giving her the **youthful features** of his own mother as he remembered her.

But there is another, more imaginative hypothesis for the youthful appearance of the Virgin. Michelangelo is picturing Mary as if she were holding, not the dead body of the **adult Jesus**, but the small body of the **baby Jesus**, capturing the moment in which Mary has a **vision** of the cruel end which awaits the child in her arms.

A curiosity

• In **1962** the *Pietà* was shipped to the **New York World's Fair** to be used as the centerpiece of the Vatican pavilion. It was the first time since its completion in 1500 that the sculpture was removed from its niche in the basilica. There was a lot of controversy about this. Many art experts and Vatican officials were opposed to moving the masterpiece. However, the request that it be sent was made by the influential New York archbishop, **Cardinal Francis Spellman**, who convinced his good friend **Pope John XXIII** to approve the request. Before the actual move, a **copy of the statue** was shipped to New York as a trial run to make sure it could be done without damage to the sculpture.

Only one other time was it necessary to move the statue. On **May 21, 1972**, a Hungarian-born Australian geologist named **Lazlo Toth** became a footnote in history when he attacked the priceless statue with a hammer. Even though the basilica was crowded with people at the time, the man was able to strike the statue **fifteen times** before he was restrained by security guards. As he was battering the sculpture with his hammer he kept yelling: *I am Jesus Christ risen from the dead!* Serious damage was done to the nose and eyelids of the Virgin and an arm was completely broken off at the elbow. The pieces were carefully collected and the statue was painstakingly and beautifully restored by experts. The priceless work of art is now protected by a **wall of bullet-proof glass**.

A curiosity

• So as not to end the story of the *Pietà* on such a negative note, let's go back to the year **1503** when **Cardinal Giuliano Della Rovere** saw the *Pietà* for the first time, just before he was elected pope in that same year, taking the name **Julius II**. One of the first things Julius did after his election was to summon the young Buonarotti to Rome to work for him. So it was the *Pietà* that brought Michelangelo to the attention and into the service of Julius II, just as the *Tempietto* did at about the same time for **Bramante**. Say what you will about Julius II, but he certainly had an aptitude for recognizing artistic talent when he saw it. A few years later he would add **Raphael** to his entourage of artists.

A close-up showing the very young face which Michelangelo gave to the mother of Jesus.

Ponte Sant'Angelo, built to give access to Hadrian's tomb, now *Castel Sant'Angelo*.
(Photo by Breck Trevino)

Chapter 19

Ponte Sant'Angelo
Not just *any* bridge

The three middle arches belong to the
original second century A.D. structure.

Ponte Sant'Angelo is the **pedestrian bridge** which leads across the **Tiber River** to **Hadrian's tomb**, later called **Castel Sant'Angelo**. The bridge was originally called *Pons Aelius* or *Pons Hadrianus* after the emperor **Aelius Hadrianus**. It was built by Hadrian in about **134 A.D.** for the purpose of connecting his tomb with the left bank of the Tiber. The bridge is made of **five arches**, the middle three of which remain from the original **second-century structure**.

Ponte Sant'Angelo, however, is probably best known for the fact that it was remodeled and decorated by **Gian Lorenzo Bernini** in the seventeenth century. Across the balustrade are **ten statues of angels**, each one holding a **symbol of the Passion of Christ** (nails, crown of thorns, etc.). The statues were executed by various followers and students of Bernini under the master's supervision and following his design. Bernini himself sculpted only two of the angels: the one holding the crown of thorns and the one with the **INRI** plaque. The originals of these are in the church of **Sant'Andrea delle Fratte** near the **Spanish Steps**.

A curiosity

• For those who may not know, the INRI across the top of the horizontal bar of the Cross of Christ stands for the Latin:

Iesus Nazarenus Rex Iudaeorum
(Jesus of Nazareth King of the Jews)

The crucifixion of Christ was carried out by **Roman soldiers**, and it was their custom to attach to the cross of the executed person a notice indicating his crime. Christ's "crime" was that he had declared himself "King of the Jews".

There is an interesting story about how the two original Bernini angels came to be in the Church of Sant'Andrea delle Fratte. **Clement IX Rospigliosi (1667-1669)** decided that the two statues were too valuable to be left out in the open on the bridge. The pope, however, did not move them into the church, but into his family home, **Palazzo Rospigliosi**, intending to transfer them to the city of **Pistoia**, his birthplace. Rospigliosi, however, died before the statues could be moved. His family, apparently fearing the wrath of the people, decided not to transfer the statues out of Rome. However, they remained in Palazzo Rospigliosi until a **nephew of Bernini** bought them and donated them to the church in **1729**. They have been in that same church ever since, one on either side of the main aisle near the main altar.

At the head of the bridge, on the opposite side from the castle, are two statues put up by **Clement VII (1523-1534)**, more than 100 years before the Bernini statues were made. On the left is **St. Peter** with the **keys**, and on the right, **St. Paul** with the **sword**.

The statues of angels and saints have been witness over the centuries to a **sinister use** of the bridge. It was often used for **public executions**, which were carried out in the center of the bridge as the **bell** on Castel Sant'Angelo sounded the death toll. The bell is still in place today, visible from the street below.

A curiosity

• One executioner during the **temporal rule** of the popes was a legend because of his **longevity** in the job. His name was **Giambattista Bugatti**, better known by his nickname of **Mastro Titta**. He was the official executioner for the Papal State from **1796** at age **seventeen** until **1864** when he retired at age **eighty-five**. In those **sixty-eight years** Mastro Titta personally carried out the execution of **516 prisoners**. Most of the executions were by **guillotine**, but Mastro Titta was equally skilled with the **hangman's noose**. The executioner had just a short walk to work as he lived in the **Borgo**, the neighborhood between Castel Sant'Angelo and the Vatican, on the tiny **Via del Campanile**. Ever since I learned about Mastro Titta, whenever I walk over the bridge or past his street, I always give a fleeting thought to him and the gruesome trade which he plied for so many decades.

The bridge seen from the terrace of Castel Sant'Angelo.
(Photo by Breck Trevino)

The tranquility and beauty of the Protestant Cemetery.

Chapter 20

A Pyramid and a Cemetery
An odd combination...or is it?

The Pyramid of Gaius Cestius as seen
from the street.

One of the best preserved monuments of ancient Rome, along with the Pantheon, is the **Pyramid of Gaius Cestius**, or *La Piramide*, as it is commonly called by the Italians. It was built during the reign of **Augustus** in **12 B.C.** as a **tomb** for an important Roman official by the name of Gaius Cestius. We know from one of three inscriptions on the face of the pyramid that Cestius held a number of important offices in the bureaucratic Roman Empire. He was a Roman magistrate, a Tribune of the Plebs and one of seven priests in charge of public banquets. Looking at the tomb he had built for himself, we can also assume that he was quite wealthy!

A curiosity

• A second inscription gives us an amazing piece of information. The tomb was built by the heirs of Cestius in the astoundingly short period of **less than 330 days**! So what prompted his relatives to rush the tomb to completion in such a short period of time? Well, it seems that Cestius didn't really trust his heirs to spend the huge sum of money it would take to build such a tomb, so he very cleverly included a clause in his will which stated that if the pyramid-tomb were not built within 330 days after his death, his heirs would NOT be allowed to claim their **considerable inheritance**!

The pyramid, built with **brick** and faced with **marble**, is enormous – about **36 meters high**, including its base. The **emperor Aurelian** made a very practical use of it by incorporating it in the **city walls** which he built in the **third century**. On the wall next to the pyramid is a plaque commemorating the **liberation of Rome** on **June 4, 1944** by allied troops. This is where they entered the city.

There is a **third inscription** close to the bottom of the structure which tells us that the monument underwent a restoration in the year **1663**. That would be during the pontificate of **Alexander VII Chigi (1655-1667)**. Uncharacteristically, the papal inscription carries only the year of the restoration and not the name of the pontiff. Notice, however, that the inscription of the Chigi pope was inscribed in letters **larger** than those of the original inscription!

The location of the pyramid is somewhat unfortunate because it stands in an area of very heavy traffic in modern Rome. It is just across from a train and subway station at the beginning of the very busy **Via Ostiensis**, the main road leading out to the town of **Ostia** and its beaches. However, just on the other side of the monument there is a very peaceful place from where to view it – the **Protestant cemetery**.

This cemetery is a real oasis of **peace** and **tranquility** in an otherwise very hectic area of Rome. In the **early nineteenth century** this was a wooded area where sheep still grazed. Little by little it came to be used as a burial place for **non-Catholics**, mostly English and German, who at that time in papal Rome were not allowed to be buried in consecrated Catholic ground. The beginning of the cemetery can be dated by its earliest known tombstone which bears the date **1738**. The cemetery grounds are now completely surrounded by a wall, thus isolating it from the confusion and noise of this zone of heavy automobile traffic.

A curiosity

• Over the entrance gate to the cemetery is a **one-word Latin inscription** attesting to the compactness of the Latin language. It reads:

RESURRECTURIS
(to those who are going to rise)

The cemetery is perhaps best known as the final resting place of the English poets **Keats** and **Shelly**. The Keats tombstone, which does not include the poet's name, carries a beautiful inscription which ends with a sentence which he himself composed:

Here lies one whose name was writ in water.

In another part of the cemetery the headstone on Shelley's grave describes him in Latin as ***Cor Cordium*** (heart of hearts).

A curiosity

• Why was Keats living in Rome, and where exactly did he live? He was in Rome on the advice of his doctors who said the milder climate of Rome would be good for his health. He lived in a rooming house at the foot of the **Spanish Steps**. Keats died in the house, from tuberculosis in **1821**. The site of the house is now a small **memorial museum** in honor of Keats and Shelly.

In the same plot with Keats is the grave of his friend **Joseph Severn**, whose tombstone reads in part:

> *To the memory of Joseph Severn, devoted friend and death-bed companion of John Keats.*

Just to the rear of, and between these two tombs is a smaller tombstone with the following poignant inscription:

> *Here also are interred the remains of Arthur Severn, the infant son of Joseph Severn, who was born 22 Nov. 1836 and accidentally killed 15 July 1837. The poet Wordsworth was present at his baptism in Rome.*

Severn returned to Rome as **British consul** from **1860-1872**. When he died in **1874** at the age of 85, he was buried next to Keats, at his own request.

Another interesting tombstone is that of **August Goethe**, the son of the famed German writer. His tombstone, like that of Keats, is **without his name**. It shows his portrait in marble, and he is identified simply as *Goethe Filius* (the son of Goethe). The inscription further tells us that the son preceded the father in death. The son died in **1830**, the father in **1832**.

Also buried here is Italian politician **Antonio Gramsci** who was instrumental in founding the Italian Communist Party when the Socialist Party split in 1921. Gramsci was arrested in **1926** by Mussolini's **fascist regime**, tried and condemned to 20 years in prison. In **1933**, for reasons of poor health, he was released to a clinic in Rome where he died in **1937**.

A curiosity

• The gravestone of Gramsci is remarkable for a Latin **grammatical error**. Near the bottom are the words: *Cinera Antonii Gramscii* (the ashes of Antonio Gramsci). As any good Latin student can tell you, *ashes* in Latin is *cineres*, not *cinera* (masculine gender, not neuter). No attempt has ever been made to correct the mistake, and by now the error is as famous as the tomb's occupant.

The tomb of Percy B. Shelley and the burial plot of Keats, Severn and Severn's infant son.

The Pyramid as seen from the cemetery grounds.

Righetto, the young hero from Trastevere, on the Janiculum hill.

Chapter 21

Righetto
A young hero from Trastevere

A close-up of Righetto.

This is the brief story of a young boy from the **Trastevere** neighborhood who became a **martyr** for the cause of the **unification of Italy**. He was one of about fifty *italianini* (little Italians), as **Giuseppe Garibaldi** called them. They were young boys, age 10-14, who risked their lives to help defend Rome and the newly declared **Italian Republic** against the French troops representing the papacy. Some of them were **drummer boys**, which put them in the front lines, directly exposed to enemy fire. Others were used as **messenger boys**, carrying instructions to various military units.

One of these boys is a figure half-way between **legend and history**. He was the leader of a band of youngsters from Trastevere like himself. His name was **Righetto** and he was **twelve years old** in 1849. Righetto had a little mongrel dog named **Sgrullarella** who was always at his master's feet. This young boy had the most dangerous job of all.

A curiosity

• So what was this dangerous task which Righetto and his young followers performed to help the cause of Italian unity? Their task, which undoubtedly saved many Italian lives, was to **disarm the cannonballs** which the French fired, by pulling out the fuses or covering them with a wet cloth before they could explode. Righetto was said to be the most skillful and courageous of all the boys who carried out this dangerous mission.

Ponte Sisto, the bridge in Trastevere near which Righetto is said to have been killed.

Fate, however, finally caught up with Righetto on **June 29, 1849**. As he attempted to disarm a cannonball on the sandy banks of the **Tiber River** below **Ponte Sisto**, it exploded in his hands, tearing apart his young body and that of his faithful companion, Sgrullarella, turning them both into the stuff of which **legends** are made.

On **February 9, 2005**, a bronze statue of this young Trastevere hero was unveiled on the Janiculum hill in a ceremony complete with political speeches and military bands. So the statue of Righetto has taken its rightful place among the busts of so many other heroes who fought and died for the Republic. Sgrullarella, as he did in life, stands between his master's feet. The Italian inscription on the base reads:

A RIGHETTO
GIOVANE TRASTEVERINO
SIMBOLO DEI RAGAZZI
CADUTI IN DIFESA DELLA GLORIOSA
REPUBBLICA ROMANA DEL 1849

(To Righetto the young Trastevere boy, symbol of the boys who fell in defense of the glorious Roman Republic of 1849).

Garibaldi called the young boys *italianini*.
(Photo by Gianfranco Mandas)

A copy of the she-wolf at the entrance to *Palazzo Senatorio*, Rome's City Hall.

Chapter 22

Romulus and Remus and the She-wolf
Symbols of Rome

The fifth-century B.C. bronze statue of
the she-wolf in the Capitoline Museums.

All over Rome you see representations of a she-wolf suckling two baby boys. The names of the boys are **Romulus** and **Remus**. They were twin brothers, and they, together with the she-wolf, are intimately connected to the **legendary story** of the founding of the city.

The story is told that in the **eighth century B.C.** the reigning king in the area which would become Rome was **Numitor**. He was overthrown by his brother **Amulius**, who then made Numitor's daughter, **Rhea Silvia**, a **Vestal Virgin** to prevent her from marrying and producing rightful heirs to the throne. Numitor himself was imprisoned.

Rhea Silvia, however, gave birth to twin boys, Romulus and Remus, fathered by the **god Mars** who had fallen in love with the beautiful young Vestal. Rhea Silvia paid a high price for breaking her vow of virginity because she was **buried alive**, as the law prescribed. Amulius then had the twins thrown into the **Tiber River**, fearing they would grow up to take revenge on him for what he had done to their grandfather. The babies, however, were washed ashore and saved by a **she-wolf** who nursed them as if they were her own pups. The boys were later found by the shepherd **Faustulus** who brought them home to be raised by himself and his wife.

When Romulus and Remus were older, Faustulus revealed to them who they really were, and he told them about the overthrow of their grandfather. The boys decided to take action, so they gathered a group of supporters and overthrew Amulius, restoring their grandfather to the throne. The twins then decided to build a settlement on the banks of the Tiber near the spot where they had been washed ashore and saved by the she-wolf.

Romulus claimed the right to be king of the new settlement, based on a **supernatural omen**, and he began to build his **city walls** on the slopes of the **Palatine hill**. In a gesture of contempt, Remus leaped over the walls, and in the ensuing struggle he was killed by his brother Romulus. The tiny settlement founded by Romulus eventually grew to become the city of **Roma**, so-named after its founder.

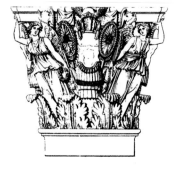

Curiosities

• The traditional date of the founding of Rome is **April 21, 753 B.C.** But how do we arrive at such an exact day as April 21? It seems to be related to the ancient festival of **Pales**, which was celebrated on this day. Pales was a **rustic spirit** in Roman religion, male according to **Varro** writing in the second century B.C., female according to **Virgil** and **Ovid** writing about a hundred years later. Ovid believed that the festival of Pales **pre-dated** the founding of Rome. In any case, at some point, the celebration of that ancient festival was adopted as the **traditional birthday** of Rome.

• Every year on April 21 the city of Rome celebrates its birthday in a big way with a series of festivities which last for three days. There is a parade of **gladiators, soldiers**, and other Roman characters, all dressed in traditional Roman garb. The parade forms in the **Circus Maximus** and makes its way past the **Colosseum** to the **Via dei Fori Imperiali** (Street of the Imperial Forums). You couldn't ask for a more authentic setting. In the evening hours there is a special illumination of the Colosseum and other famous Roman landmarks.

So the representation of two baby boys being nursed by the she-wolf has for centuries been used as the **symbol of Rome**. The most famous of the she-wolf statues is in the **Capitoline Museums**. It is an Etruscan bronze statue dating back to the **late sixth or early fifth century B.C.** (even though some scholars are now disputing its ancient Etruscan origins, dating it to the Middle Ages). The twins were not part of the original sculpture group but were added in the **sixteenth century**.

The earliest location of this statue is not known for sure, but we know that in medieval times it was located in front of the **Lateran Palace** until, in **1471**, it was donated by **Sixtus IV (1471-1484)** to the Roman people. At that time it was transferred to the **Capitoline hill** and was eventually placed in the museum where it remains today. You can see a **replica** of the famous statue high atop a column just on the left side of the **Palazzo Senatorio** in the **Piazza del Campidoglio**. But don't miss seeing the real thing when you're in Rome!

The she-wolf is found on the official gear of the Rome soccer team.

The S.P.Q.R. emblem and she-wolf at the mausoleum on the Janiculum hill.

Chapter 23

S.P.Q.R.
Ancient and modern

A modern S.P.Q.R. and the she-wolf on
one of Rome's traffic police stands.

One day on a city bus in downtown Rome I was trying to help an American couple and their two pre-teen kids who, I could tell from their conversation, were having trouble determining where to get off the bus to go to the Trevi Fountain. Once we had that problem solved, and when they learned that I was a retired Latin teacher living in Rome, they asked me: "What is this SPQR symbol that we see all over the city?"

A curiosity

• The inquisitive American tourists asked a good question because you do indeed see the SPQR symbol all over Rome, both modern and ancient. It is an **acronym** for the Latin *Senatus PopulusQue Romanus* (the Senate and Roman People). Notice that the *Que* (and) is attached to the second of the two words being joined.

In ancient times it represented the two entities (the **senate** and the **people**) which were considered supreme and sacred in Roman society. For this reason its origin probably dates to the beginning of the **Republic (510 B.C.)** when the senate and the people were considered sacrosanct. The symbol was on military banners carried into battle, proclamations issued by the government and public projects undertaken by the Roman State. It was a source of pride to the Romans. Although it continued to be used during the **Empire** beginning in **27 B.C.**, it was more because of tradition rather than conviction.

The acronym continues to be used today by **Rome's city government** on its proclamations and buildings, as well as on any project sponsored or controlled by the city. So you'll see SPQR on city buses, public drinking fountains, garbage cans, drain covers, etc. It's even the name of an **internet newsletter** sponsored by the Rome city government. Just as the **crossed keys** and the **triple crown** symbolize the papacy, so the SPQR acronym symbolizes the government of Rome, both ancient and modern. It's one way that modern Rome keeps in touch with its roots.

There is, however, a **legend** which brings the acronym back to **pre-republican** times. The story is told that it was used by a local tribe, the **Sabines**, neighbors of Rome. They used SPQR to mean: *Sabinis Populis Quis Resistet?* (Who will resist the Sabine people?). When the Romans conquered the Sabines they adopted the same acronym to mean **Senatus PopulusQue Romanus**, as if answering the rhetorical question of the Sabines.

A curiosity

• On the lighter side, in the **Middle Ages**, and even in modern times, other interpretations of the acronym were created, some **reverent**, such as the Latin: *Sanctus Petrus Quiescit Romae* (St. Peter rests in Rome), and some **irreverent**, such as the Italian: *Solo Preti Qui Regnano* (Only priests rule here), a reference to the **temporal power** of the papacy before 1870. And the **sixteenth-century Florentines**, who really disliked the Romans, reinterpreted the SPQR to read in Italian: *Sono Porci Questi Romani* (They are pigs, these Romans), or *Sono Pazzi Questi Romani* (They are crazy, these Romans)!

In any case, be prepared to see the trademark SPQR just about everywhere you turn in Rome.

A third-century A.D. S.P.Q.R. at the end of the inscription
on the Arch of Septimius Severus.

The eighteenth-century fontain in the inner courtyard of the San Cosimato complex.

Chapter 24

San Cosimato
More than meets the eye!

The church of San Cosimato at the rear of
the courtyard.

Things are not always just what they seem to be on the surface, and this is especially true in Rome. A good example of this is the unimpressive and somewhat dreary looking hospital, *il Nuovo Ospedale Regina Margherita*, on the corner of Viale di Trastevere and Via Morosini in the heart of the **Trastevere** neighborhood. It may seem dreary, but if you wander around the place you'll make some interesting and amazing discoveries. This hospital was built onto a **tenth-century Benedictine monastery** complex. Visitors to the hospital today can find some unexpected medieval and renaissance gems existing side by side with the various modern hospital departments.

There are two charming **cloisters** which were part of the monastery, one built in about **1246** and the other one during the time of **Sixtus IV Della Rovere (1471-1484)**. One wall of the first cloister is decorated with fragments of Latin inscriptions and pieces of mosaic decorations saved from the original structures. There are also some **well-preserved frescoes** on the ceiling of a short corridor just off the first cloister. This corridor leads to an open courtyard, where you will see an **ancient Roman tub** which was turned into a **fountain** in **1731**. The fountain has been recently cleaned and restored and its beautiful white marble is now sparkling. Unfortunately, they have removed the **huge goldfish** which used to swim around in the tub.

At the end of the open courtyard is the **Church of San Cosimato**, built as part of the original tenth century monastery. It was rebuilt by Sixtus IV in 1475 and restructured again in **1731**, the year the fountain was built. Just opposite the church is what used to be the main entrance to the monastery. It too has been cleaned and restored and is especially striking from the outside.

A curiosity

•   Don't go checking your Lives of the Saints to see who Cosimato was, because he didn't exist! The church was dedicated to Saints **Cosmas** and **Damian**, but the inhabitants of Trastevere, in their inimitable style, long ago fused the two names into one, creating the non-existent name **Cosimato**.

In the little church, not much more than a chapel really, is a painting of the **Madonna and Child**. Nothing unusual about that since there is probably no church in Rome without at least one painting or mosaic of the Madonna and Child. What is unusual in this case is that this is a copy of an original painting which used to be in the **old St. Peter's Basilica**.

A curiosity

• How the painting, or a copy of it, came to be in the Church of San Cosimato is explained by the following **legendary story**. In the early **sixteenth century**, this painting was stolen from St. Peter's Basilica and deprived of the precious stones which decorated it. It was then thrown into the Tiber River where it was said to have been found personally by **Leo X dei Medici (1513-1521)**. The pope had the painting set up as a little shrine on the bridge beneath which he had found it. The residents of Trastevere, however, had other ideas. They felt that the painting belonged to them, so they carried it off and attached it to a beam in their church of **San Salvatore**, no longer in existence. Later it was entrusted to the Benedictine monks at the monastery and they put it in their Church of San Cosimato. But at some point the original painting was lost and what remains to us is a copy.

The fifteenth-century cloister from the medieval Benedictine monastery.

The mausoleum on the Janiculum: the final resting place of the heroes, including some of the drummer boys.

Chapter 25

La Scalea del Tamburino
Stairway of the drummer boy

The monumental stairway at the end of
Viale Glorioso.

Sooner or later I had to write something about **my street** in the neighborhood of **Trastevere**. **Viale Glorioso** is only two blocks long, but it's a special street in a special neighborhood. Some of the regulars who hang out at Marco's **Bar Glorioso** across the street from my apartment building have nicknamed it the **Via Veneto of Trastevere!**

Viale Glorioso dead-ends into an enormous and beautiful **flight of steps** (*scalea* or *scalinata*) which leads up to the **Janiculum hill**. The stairway has the unusual name of **Scalea del Tamburino** (Stairway of the Drummer Boy). It was named to honor all the drummer boys who accompanied the Italian troops during the battles of **1849** on the Janiculum between the Italian forces of unification and the French forces of the papacy.

One of these boys, whose story is told in more than one version, was sixteen-year-old **Domenico Subiaco (1833-1849)**. Domenico was killed in the fighting on **June 3** and what follows are **two versions** of the circumstances surrounding his death. One account states that as the battle raged, the young drummer boy abandoned his drum and took up the rifle of a fallen comrade. As he began to fire at the advancing enemy, he was shot in the forehead by one of the French soldiers. He is said to have fallen and died **near a stairway**.

A second version places the action at the **Porta San Pancrazio** (San Pancrazio gate) at the top of the Janiculum. Here the Italians were trying to hold back the advancing French troops. Young Domenico, abandoning his drum, climbed to the top of the gate and called for his comrades to pass him **loaded rifles**. Although he was totally exposed to enemy fire, he managed to fire several shots before he was struck by a French bullet. The force of the blow pushed him over the edge of the gate and he fell to his death.

It is thought that perhaps these two versions of the death of a drummer boy have been drawn from the lives of several such boys, a composite account. In any case, the staircase was not dedicated to any single drummer boy, such as Domenico Subiaco, but to ALL the drummer boys who participated in the action.

A curiosity

• Domenico himself is remembered by an **engraved inscription** in his home village of **Ripi**, south of Rome, while the nearby city of **Frosinone** has placed a **bronze statue** of him in the main square of the city. So the young hero, whatever his story, has not been forgotten.

But the *Scalea del Tamburino* is also known for another, more modern character. Who can forget the very successful Italian westerns, the so-called **spaghetti westerns** of the 1960's, directed by the great **Sergio Leone** (born in Rome in **1929** and died in Rome in **1989**)? His films introduced a **new genre** of movie which enjoyed immediate success at the box office. The director lived just off the scalinata at the end of Viale Glorioso. Reportedly, it was one of his **favorite haunts** in Rome.

A curiosity

•   In **1990** the City of Rome set up at the bottom of the stairway a marker which carries the following words of the late director:

> *Il mio modo di vedere le cose talvolta è ingenuo, un po' infantile,*
> *ma sincero, come i bambini della scalinata di Viale Glorioso.*

> (My way of seeing things is sometimes naive, a little childish,
> but sincere, like the children of the stairway of Viale Glorioso).

Hats off to Domenico Subiaco and all the Italian drummer boys of 1849, as well as to the late lamented Sergio Leone!

The plaque at the base of the stairway, recalling the words
of Italian film director, Sergio Leone.

The central doors of the Basilica of St. John Lateran are the original doors of the Senate House.

Chapter 26

The Senate House
The seat of power

The exterior of the Senate House in the
Roman Forum.

The **Senate House** in the **Roman Forum** was the seat of power of the Roman Empire for centuries. Here is where decisions were made which affected the lives of millions of people in the vast territory ruled by the Romans. The history of the building itself is interesting because of the many famous people who had a hand in building and restoring it over the centuries.

The building which we see today is not the original Senate House. It is a re-construction by the **emperor Diocletian** after a disastrous fire in **283 A.D.** However, it seems to have followed closely the plan of the earlier structure, the **Curia Iulia**, named after **Julius Caesar** who began its construction in **44 B.C.** After Caesar's assassination, the Curia was finished by **Augustus** in **29 B.C.**

This is the **best-preserved** building in the Roman Forum because in **630 A.D.** it was converted into the Church of St. Hadrian by **Pope Honorius I (625-638)**. This was just a few years after the **Pantheon** had undergone the same transformation into a church by **Boniface IV (608-615)**. An amazing discovery was made centuries later when the church of St. Hadrian was dismantled in **1935-1938**: the original marble floor of the Senate House was discovered, **perfectly preserved**, beneath the floor of the church. It consists of green and red porphyry on backgrounds of yellow and purple marble. It is really a spectacular sight, one of the highlights of the Roman Forum.

A curiosity

• The huge **bronze doors** currently on the building are **seventeenth-century replicas** of the originals. What happened to the original doors is an interesting story involving a pope and his very famous architect. In **1660 Francesco Borromini** was doing restyling work on the **Basilica of St. John Lateran**. The pope at the time, **Alexander VII Chigi (1655-1667)** ordered Borromini to remove the doors from the Curia and install them on the basilica. The replicas were made shortly afterwards and placed on the Senate House. The original doors had to be trimmed down to fit the somewhat smaller frame of the Lateran church, and when they were being adapted, a **coin** of the **emperor Domitian (81-96 A.D.)** was found in the core. The **stars** that you see decorating the original doors today were added when they were installed in the church. They represent the stars on the Chigi pope's family **coat of arms**.

Only on special occasions are visitors allowed to walk around inside the Curia, but you can get a good idea of how magnificent it must have been by standing at the open doors and looking in. At the far end you see two doors which lead into the **Forum of Julius Caesar**, serving to connect it with the original Roman Forum. Between these two doors is a **low platform** which once held an altar and a statue of **Winged Victory** donated to the Senate by Augustus. Today on this platform we see a statue of a **Roman** wearing a **toga**, the official dress of the adult, male Roman citizen. Some experts believe that the statue dates to the **Imperial age** and possibly represents the **emperor Trajan (98-117)**.

It rests on a base which may well have been the one on which the ancient statue of Winged Victory stood. There are also two **marble balustrades** housed in the Curia today. They were found nearby in the Forum and were placed in the Senate House for safekeeping. Still visible in the interior on either side of a spacious aisle are **marble tiers** which provided space for **three hundred senators**.

The interior of the Senate House showing the original marble floor.

The eighteenth-century Trevi Fountain in the center of Rome.

Chapter 27

The Trevi Fountain
Don't forget to throw in your coin!

The central part of the Trevi Fountain.

The **Trevi Fountain** is probably the best known and most popular of Rome's many fountains. It was made even more famous by the **Fellini** movie *La Dolce Vita*. Who can forget the scene of **Anita Ekberg** prancing around in the fountain in the wee hours of the morning! Other films have used the Trevi as background or as centerpiece, such as the 1950's movie *Three Coins in the Fountain*. And speaking of coins, everyone knows that if you throw a coin into the fountain, your return to Rome is assured.

As with other monuments built prior to 1870 in Rome, this one also is owed to the papacy. In 1732 **Clement XII (1730-1740)** sponsored a competition for the commission to build the fountain. It was won by Rome architect **Nicola Salvi** with his very Bernini-like design. The handsome Latin inscription at the top of the fountain tells us about its origin and its wholesome waters.

CLEMENS XII PONT. MAX.
AQUAM VIRGINEM
COPIA ET SALUBRITATE COMMENDATAM
CULTU MAGNIFICO ORNAVIT
ANNO DOMINI MDCCXXXV PONTIF. VI

(Clement XII, Supreme Pontiff, adorned with magnificent style the Virgin Water, recommended because of its plentifulness and its wholesomeness, in the year of the Lord 1735, the sixth year of his pontificate)

A curiosity

• The fountain was incomplete at Clement's death in 1740 and was finished under his successor, **Benedict XIV (1740-1758)** who added a **second inscription** in huge gold letters telling us that he finished the job. However, the fountain was not dedicated until **1762** by **Clement XIII (1758-1769)** who somehow found a spot for a **third inscription** with his name on it. So three consecutive popes left their mark (literally!) on the Trevi Fountain!

The tradition of a fountain on this site goes back 300 years before the present structure was built. **Nicholas V (1447-1455)** had a small fountain built here to give the Romans the opportunity of taking the clear, clean water home for drinking and bathing. Rome was just emerging from the **Middle Ages** at this time in its history and there was precious little clean water available to the population, so the building of that small fountain was an important event in the life of the city.

The fountain is fed by the waters of the *Acqua Vergine*, an **aqueduct** built by the Roman consul **Agrippa in 19 B.C.** to bring water to the set of baths which he had built nearby.

A curiosity

• The waters are called *Acqua Vergine* (virgin water) because when Agrippa and his soldiers were searching for the water source up in the hills outside of Rome, a young girl who lived in the area showed them where it was. This explains the two **relief carvings** on the face of the fountain, one showing the girl pointing out the water to the soldiers, and the other showing Agrippa inspecting the plans of the aqueduct, with the aqueduct itself visible in the background.

At the top of the fountain is the **papal coat of arms** of Clement XII. Just below that is the main inscription flanked by **four statues** representing the **four seasons**. In the center is a statue of **Neptune**, god of the sea, in his chariot pulled by two horses lead by two Tritons.

Salvi cleverly designed the chariot of Neptune as a **seashell**, and notice that one of the horses is **calm** and one is **agitated**, representing the two possible conditions of the sea. The statues on either side of Neptune represent **Health** and **Abundance**, reflecting the quality and quantity of the water.

Curiosities:

• The story is told that, when the fountain was under construction, there was a **barber shop** on the right side just across the street from the fountain. The barber was very critical of the architect's design and not at all shy about expressing his criticisms. Salvi got a little tired of this, so one day he carved onto the fountain a large **ornamental vase** in a spot where it effectively **blocked the view** of the fountain from the barber shop! The barber shop no longer exists, but the vase is still there where Salvi put it.

• On one corner of the square, across from the fountain, is the **Church of Santi Vincenzo e Anastasio**. It was called the **pontifical parish church** because of its proximity to the **Quirinal Palace**, the summer residence of the popes. There used to be a **bizarre custom** of burying the **heart** and **lungs** of deceased pontiffs in the crypt of this, their parish church. The practice went on for over **300 years**, beginning with **Sixtus V in 1590** and ending with **Leo XIII in 1903**, a total of thirty popes!

The Tiber Island on December 7, 2005. We had a little rain that week!

Chapter 28

The Tiber Island
Legends and facts

The Fatebenefratelli hospital
on the Tiber Island.

The **Tiber River** flows in a twisting motion through the very heart of Rome, a silent witness to incredible events which have taken place here over the centuries. One of the most characteristic sights on the river is the *Isola Tiberina*, an island in the **form of a ship**, which is one of the oldest landmarks in Rome, older than the city itself. The island is connected to the mainland by a bridge on either side of it, and if you look at an aerial photograph of the area you will see that the two bridges appear to be **gigantic oars** powering the "ship" upstream. An **obelisk** in the middle of the island adds to this illusion; it appears to be the **mast of the ship**.

One of these bridges, the *Pons Cestius*, was built in **46 B.C.**, but was completely rebuilt in **1892**. The other one, however, the *Pons Fabricius*, is still its original self from **62 B.C.** In fact, it is the only continually used Roman bridge left in the city. The two bridges account for the **alternate name** which the Romans gave to the island: *Inter Duos Pontes* (between two bridges). The original inscription from 62 B.C. is still visible on one of the arches of the *Pons Fabricius*.

L. Fabricius. C. F. Cur. Viar. Faciundum. Coeravit

(Lucius Fabricius, son of Gaius, superintendent of roads,
took care that it be built)

The Tiber Island has been associated with the work of **healing** ever since the Romans dedicated a temple here to the Greek god of healing, **Aesculapius**, in **291 B.C.** The medical connection and the work of healing continue today at the *Fatebenefratelli* hospital which was established on the island in **1584** by **St. John of God**.

A curiosity

• There was a big celebration at the hospital in 2005 to mark the **thirtieth anniversary** of the founding of its **maternity ward**, which has become the most popular place in Rome for giving birth. It seems that the Romans will do just about anything to have their children born on the island. In the thirty years between 1975 and 2005, it recorded **73,892 births**, an average of **2,429 every year**. The record year for births is **1998** when **3,570 babies** were born. It is estimated that one out of seven Romans alive today first saw the light of day at the *Fatebenefratelli*!

The reason why the Romans chose this particular site to build their temple to Aesculapius is explained by a **legendary story**. Rome had been struck by a **devastating plague** in **293 B.C.**, and since the Roman gods seemed helpless against the pestilence, the Romans decided to seek help from the Greek god of healing. They sent a delegation to the city of Epidaurus to bring back to Rome a **statue of the god** to put in the temple which they planned to build in his honor. When the ship was returning from Greece carrying the statue, and just as it was passing the Tiber Island, a **snake**, an animal **sacred to Aesculapius**, slithered off the boat and into the river. The snake was seen as it swam ashore on the island and **wrapped itself around the trunk of a tree**. The Romans took this as a sign that the temple should be built on the island, and so it was. This story also explains why to this day the **symbol of medicine and healing** is a snake wrapped around the trunk of a tree. At the back of the island you can still see this symbol in stone dating to the **first century B.C.**

In the **tenth century** a church dedicated to **St. Bartholomew the Apostle** was built on the site of the temple of Aesculapius. The inscription across the façade of the church states:

In hac basilica requiescit corpus Sancti Bartholomei Apostoli

(In this church rests the body of St. Bartholomew the Apostle)

A curiosity

• Inside the church, in a side chapel to the right of the main altar, you will see an unusual sight. A **cannonball** is imbedded in the side wall of the chapel! In 1849 when the Italians were fighting the French papal troops on the **Janiculum hill** overlooking the Tiber Island, a stray cannonball hit the church and was embedded in the wall of the chapel. Although the church was filled with worshipers at the time, no one was hurt, so the Italians called it the **miracle cannonball**. They left it sticking in the wall of the chapel right where it had landed.

Pons Fabricius, built in the first century B.C., still has its original inscription.

It's a very pleasant walk across the island from one bridge to the other. And just across the bridges are two of Rome's most interesting neighborhoods. Off the *Pons Fabricius* is the historic **Jewish Ghetto**

131

and **Synagogue**, while the *Pons Cestius* on the opposite side leads to the old **Trastevere** neighborhood.

A curiosity

• The Tiber Island was the site of an **interesting festival**, now abandoned, the *Sagra dei cocomeri* (Watermelon Festival). It took place every year on **August 24**, the feast day of St. Bartholomew. For the occasion, the piazza in front of the church would be lined with scores of **whole watermelons**. At a given moment the watermelons would be thrown into the Tiber. This was the signal for dozens of *ragazzetti* (young boys) to dive into the river and challenge each other to get possession of one of the prized watermelons. You can imagine the scene!

The boys took the challenge very seriously and the battle for the watermelons was fierce. So much so that there were often **serious injuries** among the young participants. Because of the danger involved, the colorful **watermelon battle** was discontinued after the unification of Italy in 1870. Even though this particular festival no longer exists, the **luscious, cold, red watermelons** are sold today by the slice all over the city – a welcome sight during the hot summer months.

The Church of St, Bartholomew where the apostle is buried.
(Photo by Gianfranco Mandas)

Pons Cestius joins the Tiber Island to Trastevere. (Photo by Gianfranco Mandas)

The tomb of Julius II: Moses. (Photo by Gianfranco Mandas)

Chapter 29

The Tomb of Julius II
Michelangelo's unfinished masterpiece

A close-up of part of the tomb
of Julius II.

Julius II Della Rovere (1503-1513) was a famous patron of the arts and he had three very famous renaissance artists working at the same time in the Vatican under his patronage. **Bramante** was hired as chief architect of the new St. Peter's Basilica, **Raphael** was employed to decorate the papal apartments, and **Michelangelo** received the commission to paint the frescoes on the ceiling of the Sistine Chapel. Not a shabby trio, I would say!

These three artists have given us incredibly beautiful works of art, sculpture and architecture, but the one which promised to be the most impressive and extravagant of all was never completed – the **tomb of Julius II** by Michelangelo. The pope had envisioned a **massive funeral monument** to himself in the very center of St. Peter's Basilica. Michelangelo's first sketches incorporated as many as **forty statues** on the monument. Only a small part of the tomb was ever finished, but that small part includes a statue which is considered to be one of Michelangelo's greatest masterpieces. If you think you've never heard of the tomb of Julius II, think again, because you have certainly heard of this one statue which is the centerpiece of the unfinished tomb: **Michelangelo's Moses**.

A curiosity

• So why was the pope's tomb never completed? After all, Michelangelo worked on it off and on for **almost forty years**. It seems that Julius himself lost interest in it, perhaps because it was going to take so long to complete, and he preferred that Michelangelo work on other projects, such as the **frescoes of the Sistine Chapel**. After the death of Julius, his successors kept Michelangelo busy with other commissions, so the tomb was never finished as Michelangelo had planned it. We are left with only **seven** of those forty statues first envisioned by the artist.

There has always been speculation about the **pose** given by Michelangelo to the statue of Moses, his "body language", so to speak. It was psychoanalyst **Sigmund Freud** in 1914 who first gave a plausible and realistic explanation of the posture of Moses. Freud's hypothesis is that Moses is depicted at the moment in which, **having received the tablets of the Law**, he becomes aware that his people have given themselves to **idolatry** by **worshipping the golden calf**, and he is in the act of **rising from his seated position**. His head and eyes are turned to his left as if he has been attracted by some unexpected uproar. His left foot is poised behind him to push as he prepares to stand up, and at the same time his right arm **grasps the tablets of the Law** tightly to his side as if to keep them from falling when he stands up.

The tomb is not in St. Peter's Basilica as Julius had wished, but in the **Basilica of San Pietro in Vincoli** (St. Peter in Chains), so-called because it contains a **set of chains** which tradition says are the ones which bound St. Peter when he was a prisoner in Rome.

Restoration of the Tomb

The tomb recently underwent a **major and lengthy restoration** which was completed in late 2003, the result of which shows the sculpture group in all its brilliance, just as Michelangelo himself would have seen it. Not only did it undergo a **thorough cleaning**, but perhaps even more exciting is that it was given a different **architectural perspective** believed to be as Michelangelo himself originally executed it. At the very top of the monument is an **arch** which was filled in with frames and glass in a **seventeenth-century restoration**. These frames and the glass have now been removed. Also, the **four small windows** above the figure of the rising pontiff, which had been closed in the seventeenth century restoration, have been restored to their original open look.

A startling discovery

There are six statues alongside and above the statue of Moses, and for centuries it was believed that the Moses and the **two statues flanking it** were the only ones of the group actually carved by the master. However, during this latest restoration of the sculpture, an **amazing discovery** was made about the **statue of Julius II** which is located above the Moses and which depicts the pope in what appears to be a **reclining position**. What the experts found led them to declare that the reclining statue of the pontiff was carved by the **hand of Michelangelo himself**. They based this **bold declaration** on the following findings:

—Unmistakable **traces of chisel marks** were found on the statue. **Only Michelangelo** had the skill to be able to use the chisel directly on the marble where an errant chip would be an **irreversible mistake**. Other sculptors used a **rasp**, a tool used to scrape, as opposed to the chisel, used to chip.

—They found that the figure of Julius is not just reclining, it is in a **rising motion**, similar to two rising figures in Michelangelo's **Last Judgment fresco** in the Sistine Chapel.

—The **anatomical detail**, particularly of the hands, is much more pronounced on the statue of the pope than on the others in the group. Such detail is typical of Michelangelo.

—The **back of the statue** was discovered to have been carved, as well as other places that would have been very difficult to reach, and would never have been seen by the public. We know that this was a technique used by Michelangelo and by very few other sculptors.

The tomb of Julius II by Michelangelo. The statue of Moses is at the center.
(Photo by Breck Trevino)

"A small column for a small piazza". The column in front of the church
of San Francesco a Ripa.

Chapter 30

Trastevere and Pius IX
A little papal humor

Palazzo dei Tabacchi: The tobacco
factory of Pius IX in Piazza Mastai.

You would probably never expect that a **pope** would have a **tobacco factory** built. Well, think again, because **Pius IX Mastai-Ferretti (1846-1878)** did just that in 1863. The imposing palazzo, the work of **Antonio Sarti**, is called *Fabbrica dei Tabacchi* (the Tobacco Factory). It stands in the square named after the pope, **Piazza Mastai**, located on the main thoroughfare of the Trastevere neighborhood, *Viale di Trastevere*. The handsome Latin inscription across the width of the façade tells the story.

PIUS . IX . P . M . OFFICINAM . NICOTIANIS . FOLIIS .
ELABORANDIS . A . SOLO . EXTRUXIT . ANNO . MDCCCLXIII

(Pius IX, Supreme Pontiff, erected this factory from its foundations in the year 1863 for producing tobacco.)

Two years later, in **1865**, the **fountain** was built by architect **Andrea Busiri Vici** to decorate the square directly in front of the palazzo. A set of three steps leads up to the **octagonal-shaped basin** which bears the **papal coat of arms** and the inscription:

PIUS IX P.M. ANNO DOMINI MDCCCLXV PONT. XX

(Pius IX, Supreme Pontiff, in the year of the Lord 1865,
the twentieth of his pontificate.)

A curiosity

• When Papa Mastai visited the palazzo shortly after it was finished, he was a little disappointed at the final result. He complained that the **main entrance was too small** in proportion to the size of the whole building. However he accepted the "defect" good naturedly with the following **witty remark** immediately after entering the building through the door in question: *Now that I have entered through the WINDOW, will you please show me the DOOR!*

VICOLO R.XIII
DEI
TABACCHI

The little street so-named because
it flanks the tobacco factory.

Trastevere is a neighborhood **full of curiosities** for those who know where to look for them. What follows is the story of one of those curiosities which is not likely to be found in most guidebooks. It concerns a **column** in the square in front of one of Trastevere's historic churches, the thirteenth-century **Church of San Francesco a Ripa**.

The **Franciscan monastery** attached to the church is said to have hosted **St. Francis of Assisi** on one of his trips to Rome. The church itself displays a magnificent late work by **Gian Lorenzo Bernini**: a statue of the **Blessed Ludovica Albertoni**, sculpted by the artist in 1675 at his age 75.

But the church and the statue are not the curiosity. In the square in front of the church is a **small column** which sometimes goes unnoticed because of the jumble of parked cars around it. Almost no one stops to look at the column before going into the church, and yet there is an interesting and humorous story about the column and its **Latin inscription**.

It was Pius IX who donated the column in 1847 to the Franciscan monks and their parishioners as ornamentation in front of their church. However, after the column was completed and set up in the square, the monks and their parishioners were offended, complaining that the dimensions of the column were too modest. *It can't be*, they murmured among themselves, *that such a small column be placed in front of such an important church*!

Somehow, their complaint reached the ears of the pontiff himself who smiled and said: *A small column for a small piazza*! Then he had the following dedication sculpted on the base of the column:

PIUS . IX . PONT . MAX .
COLUMNAM
AREAE AMPLITUDINI
PAREM
DONAVIT
AN . M . DCCC . XLVII

(Pius IX, Supreme Pontiff, donated this column,
equal to the size of the piazza, in the year 1847.)

Another example of the **sharp wit** and **sense of humor** of Papa Mastai!

The obelisk in the middle of St. Peter's Square.

Chapter 31

The Vatican Obelisk
Witness to a martyrdom

The obelisk stands between two
Bernini-designed fountains.

It stands **twenty-five meters high**, but with its base and its cross at the top, it reaches beyond **forty meters**. We are talking about the magnificent **red granite obelisk** which has dominated St. Peter's Square for over four hundred years. The obelisk, however, is not Roman, nor has it always been in its present location. The **emperor Caligula** ordered the obelisk to be brought to Rome from **Alexandria, Egypt in 37 A.D.** to decorate the center of his Circus.

A curiosity

• It was no small task to transport **three hundred tons of granite** across the sea from Alexandria to Rome. In fact, a ship was built especially for this job. The ship was never used again, but was sunk in the harbor of **Ostia** by the **emperor Claudius** as a foundation for a pier and lighthouse.

It was in this Circus of Caligula, later called the Circus of Nero, that **St. Peter** was crucified in **67 A.D.** Since the obelisk was there at the time, it is very possible that it was the last thing that the Apostle laid his eyes on before he died. For over **1,500 years** the obelisk remained in its original location which turned out to be along the left side of the first St. Peter' Basilica.

In **1585**, as the new St. Peter's Basilica was nearing completion, **Pope Sixtus V Peretti (1585-1590)** decided to have the obelisk moved some 300 yards to the center of the square in front of the basilica. The papal architect, **Domenico Fontana**, was put in charge of the monumental task which took an entire year to complete, as the work began in **September, 1585** and concluded in **September, 1586**. Fontana employed some **800 men, 140 horses** and **47 cranes** to move it. Every movement of the workers was regulated by a trumpet blast, so the pope had ordered that there be **absolute silence** in the square so that the workers could hear the trumpet.

Curiosities

• There is a legendary story about the architect Fontana, who had a healthy fear of the quick-tempered pontiff. The story says that Fontana kept a horse saddled just off the square, ready for a **quick getaway** in case the obelisk would fall and shatter into thousands of pieces!

• Yet another story tells how the order for silence in the square during the transfer of the obelisk was under **pain of death**. The no-nonsense Sixtus is said to have had a **gallows** erected in the square, in full view of the spectators, for the immediate carrying-out of the execution of anyone who broke the silence and in any way impeded the work.

• But the best known story (and some say it is not legend, but fact) is the one about the **sailor from Genova** who was in the crowd of people watching the massive operation of the moving of the obelisk. He noticed that the ropes holding the obelisk were about to snap because of the friction. **Risking his life**, he broke the rule of silence, yelling out: "Water to the ropes!" The water was applied and the ropes held. The obelisk was safely set into its position. Far from punishing the man for breaking the rule, Sixtus was so grateful to the sailor for having saved the obelisk that he granted his family the privilege of supplying St. Peter's with **palms for Palm Sunday**, a privilege supposedly still enjoyed by his descendants.

There is a marker in the pavement on the left side of the basilica just beyond the **Arch of the Bells** which indicates the spot where the obelisk stood for over 1,500 years before it was moved into the square. The extraordinary transfer of the obelisk to the center of the square is recalled by the following **Latin inscription** on the base of the obelisk:

Sixtus V Pont. Max
Cruci Invictae
Obeliscum Vaticanum
Ab Impura Superstitione
Expiatum Iustius
Et Felicius Consecravit
Anno MDLXXXVI Pont. II

(Sixtus V, Supreme Pontiff, more justly and more happily dedicated to the unconquered Cross the Vatican Obelisk, purified from its unclean superstition, in the year 1586, the second of his pontificate.)

A curiosity

• Originally, at the top of the obelisk there was a **bronze globe** which was said to contain **the bones of Julius Caesar**. However, when the obelisk was moved, the globe was taken down and found to be empty. Sixtus then donated the globe to the city of Rome, and it was put in the **Palazzo dei Conservatori** of the **Capitoline Museums**. In place of the globe at the top of the obelisk, the pontiff set up a bronze cross containing **relics of the True Cross**.

147

The Arch of Titus in the Roman Forum. Both Titus and Vespasian
are mentioned in the inscription.

Chapter 32

Vespasian
A colossal gift

A bust of the emperor Vespasian in the
Palazzo Massimo Museum.

Titus Flavius Vespasianus, born in the **year 9 A.D.**, ruled as Roman emperor for ten years from **69** until his death in **79**. He was one of the few emperors to die a natural death following a short illness. His middle name, *Flavius*, is the name of his extended family, or clan. He was the first of the **Flavian emperors** and would be followed by his sons, **Titus** and **Domitian**. Vespasian's road to power was a bloody one, particularly in the year **69**, known in history as the **Year of the Four Emperors**.

It all began in **68** when the Roman governor of Spain, **Galba**, realized that **Nero** was planning to have him murdered. Galba, however, beat his boss to the punch. He promised **financial favors** to the soldiers of the **Praetorian Guard**, the imperial bodyguards, who then forced Nero to commit suicide on **June 9, 68**. Galba then marched into Rome and was declared emperor by the **Roman Senate**. He would be the first of the four emperors of 69.

On **January 9, 69**, Galba himself was killed by members of the Praetorian Guard who had been won over, once again, by **financial promises**, this time from another general, **Otho** whom the Guard promptly hailed as emperor on January 15. Number two in the year of the four.

Otho, however, was soon challenged by **Vitellius**, and on April 16, realizing that he was losing the battle for power, Otho stabbed himself to death. Thus Vitellius became emperor number three in the year of the four.

Finally, Vespasian, a very successful Roman general and very popular with his soldiers, became the fourth Roman emperor in the year 69 when his supporters executed Vitellius in Rome. The imperial blood bath was over and Vespasian would have a successful ten-year rule. But history will always record the year 69 as the Year of the Four Emperors: Galba, Otho, Vitellius and Vespasian.

A curiosity

• As a general, Vespasian had an on-again-off-again relationship with Nero. He never really liked him and was bored by Nero's histrionic performances. One amusing anecdote about their relationship tells how, in 66, Vespasian accompanied Nero to Greece. There he fell into **imperial disfavor**, not because of some military decision or blunder, but because **he fell asleep** at one of Nero's performances!

Vespasian's name inevitably comes up when the **Colosseum** is mentioned because he is the emperor who had it built. He literally had **Nero's private lake** drained and he built the Colosseum on that spot. It was his gift – a colossal one – to the people of Rome. He didn't see it completed and inaugurated in **80** because he died in **79**. The work was finished by his son and successor, Titus. The official name of the Colosseum is the **Flavian Amphitheater**, so called from the clan name of Vespasian and Titus.

Vespasian was leading the Roman army in a battle to subdue the **revolt of the Jews** at the time he was named emperor. He left the battle immediately and returned to Rome, leaving his son Titus in charge of the army. Titus eventually put down the Jewish revolt and **sacked the city of Jerusalem in 70**. He and Vespasian then celebrated a **Triumph** together, marching through the **Roman Forum** with the spoils of war and the prisoners taken in Jerusalem.

After the death of Titus in **81**, his brother and successor, Domitian, had a **triumphal arch** built in the Forum in honor of that victory. The arch, known as the **Arch of Titus**, stands there today at one end of the Forum near the family's other famous monument, the Colosseum. On the side of the arch facing the Colosseum you can admire the **original Latin inscription**, still intact. It contains the names of both father and son, and reads as follows:

SENATUS
POPULUSQUE ROMANUS
DIVO TITO D. VESPASIANI F.
VESPASIANO AUGUSTO

(The Senate and Roman People to the Divine Titus Vespasian Augustus, Son of the Divine Vespasian).

The Colosseum and the Arch of Titus seen from the Palatine hill.

A view of the tiny *Vicolo dell'Atleta* in the Trastevere neighborhood.

Chapter 33

Vicolo dell'Atleta
Athlete Lane

Vicolo dell'Atleta, so-named because the statue of *Apoxyomenos* was found here.

The streets of my **Trastevere** neighborhood are not exactly in what you would call a grid layout. On the contrary, they are a maze of twisting and turning streets, some of them too narrow for automobile traffic. It's literally impossible to "walk around the block". And this is precisely what makes the area so fascinating. You have a clue that you will be dealing with a **small street** when the name is preceded by *vicolo* (lane) instead of *via* (street).

And the **names** of the streets often have an interesting, even historical significance, not only in Trastevere, but in all of Rome. Many of them carry the names of Italian heroes, like **Via Garibaldi**, or cities, like **Via Roma**, or historic dates in the history of Italy, like **Via XX Settembre**. Trastevere's **Vicolo dell'Atleta** (Athlete Lane), you would think, must surely have a story behind it, and you would be correct.

In the **fourth century B.C.** a bronze statue of an athlete was made by **Lysippus**, one of the greatest Greek sculptors of his century. The athlete is not represented **in action**, but rather during the **cooling down period** after his competition, probably a foot race.

A curiosity

• To purify their bodies, ancient Greek and Roman athletes, but not only athletes, would rub themselves with **oil** and then scrape the oil off with an instrument called a **strigil**. This was a common practice at the **Roman baths**. This particular statue by Lysippus depicts the athlete as he "strigils" the oil off his body, probably after soaking himself a while in the baths.

Unfortunately, the original fourth-century bronze statue has been lost. However, the statue is mentioned by the **first century A.D.** Roman writer **Pliny the Elder**, so we know it was known at that time. More importantly, Pliny also tells us that a **marble copy** of the original bronze statue was made in Rome during his lifetime, and he left us a good description of it.

For centuries the Roman copy was also lost and all we had was Pliny's description of it. Then in **1849** a marble statue was discovered, buried beneath a tiny street in the Trastevere neighborhood near the **Tiber Island**. The statue was immediately recognized by experts as the **Roman copy** of the Greek original described by Pliny in the first century A.D.

A curiosity

• Since the Roman statue was inspired by a Greek original, it was decided to give it a Greek name. It's called **Apoxyomenos**, meaning "a man scraping himself". In 1849 Rome was still under **papal control**, so guess who claimed the statue! Yes, it was promptly hurried off to the **Vatican Museums** where we can admire it today.

The statue is displayed very effectively in the middle of its own little **round vestibule**, like the **David** in Florence, so that the visitor can walk all the way around it and admire it from all sides. In honor of this important discovery, the name of the tiny street in Trastevere where the statue was found in 1849 was changed to **Vicolo dell'Atleta** (Athlete Lane).

The statue of *Apoxyomenos*, now in the Vatican Museums.

This is the view which the Finnish ambassador enjoys from his back porch!

Chapter 34

Villa Lante
A breathtaking view

The sixteenth-century Villa Lante, now
the Finnish Embassy to the Vatican.

I had passed in front of this small but beautiful building literally hundreds of times, either on foot or on the 870 bus headed down the **Janiculum hill** towards the city center. This entire area offers a **spectacular view** of the city below, but I had often wished to be able to enjoy that sight from the terrace of that palazzo. At an extraordinary opening to the public one weekend I stood in line for two and a half hours to get in for a thirty minute visit, but it was worth it for both the view and the historical information.

The building in question is **Villa Lante**, a renaissance palace built in the **early 1500's** for **Baldassare Turini**, an eminent personality in renaissance Rome. Turini had a very close relationship with the Medici family of Florence, and when **Cardinal Giovanni de'Medici** was elected as **Pope Leo X (1513-1521)**, Turini was given a high position in the papal entourage. He also knew most of the great renaissance artists of his day, including **Raphael**. The palazzo was, in fact, built by **Giulio Romano**, a brilliant young student of Raphael. It was Romano's first major project.

In 1551 the villa was sold to the **Lante family**, hence the name Villa Lante. In **1837** it was acquired by the **Sisters of the Sacred Heart** and turned into a kindergarten school.

A curiosity

• The good sisters judged some of the **frescoes** in the palazzo to be a little too risqué for the kiddies, so they had the offending scenes removed. They were bought by a private individual and are today stored in **Palazzo Zuccari** in Rome, near the **Spanish Steps**.

In **1950** the villa was purchased by the **government of Finland**, and is used by that country today as its **Embassy to the Holy See**, and as the **Roman Institute of Finland**. One couldn't ask for a more spectacular location.

A curiosity

• In one of the rooms, which I unfortunately did not see on my visit, there is preserved a historic bit of **graffiti** from the **sixteenth century**. It reads, in the Italian of that day, *a di 6 de maggio 1527 / fo la presa de Roma* (on the sixth day of May, 1527, was the capture of Rome). It refers to the disastrous **Sack of Rome** by German mercenary troops on that date. Someone, perhaps a workman in the villa, left that short message for posterity.

Villa Lante, barely completed in 1527, somehow escaped the wrath of the marauding troops and survived the infamous Sack of Rome, perhaps because it was a little out of the way, up on the hill. It survived more warfare in **1848** when the first battles of the **Italian War of Unification** were fought on the Janiculum hill. There are reminders all around the villa of the fighting that took place up here in those historic battles, including a monument to **Giuseppe Garibaldi** and the tomb of his wife **Anita**. There are also dozens of **marble busts** marked with the names of many of the individuals who fought with Garibaldi.

The rear of Villa Lante looks out over the city of Rome. (Photo by Gianfranco Mandas)

The view of Rome from the terrace of the Victor Emmanuel Monument.

Chapter 35

Il Vittoriano
The wedding cake

The tomb of the unknown soldier with its
military honor guard.

Everybody who has ever come to Rome has seen the enormous **white limestone monument** in Piazza Venezia, the geographical center of Rome. The official name of this building is the **Victor Emmanuel Monument**, referred to in Italian as *Il Vittoriano*. It looms high above the piazza and dwarfs all the other buildings in the vicinity. The construction of the monument has been criticized for this reason and for the fact that a part of the **Capitoline hill** had to be cut away to make room for it. Some medieval and renaissance buildings were destroyed or altered in the process. The monument has also been given various **nicknames** over the years, including the **wedding cake** and **Mussolini's typewriter**. (The Duce's office was in Palazzo Venezia just in front of the monument).

The *Vittoriano* was begun in **1885** as a monument in honor of **Victor Emmanuel II**, the first king of a united Italy. It was inaugurated in **1911** by his grandson, **Victor Emmanuel III**, although it was not fully completed until **1935**.

A curiosity

• Why did they inaugurate the monument some **24 years** before its completion? Well, in 1911 the country was celebrating the **fiftieth anniversary** of the establishment of the modern State of Italy in **1861**, so it seemed an appropriate occasion to inaugurate a monument to its first Head of State.

In **1970** a ten-foot-high **iron fence** was set up across the front of the monumental stairway to block public access to it after a **terrorist bomb explosion**. It remained closed for **over 30 years** until the president of Italy, **Carlo Azeglio Ciampi** had it reopened to the public in **2001**. In fact, President Ciampi is credited with restoring the dignity of the monument and instilling in the Italians a sense of pride for what it represents, which is illustrated by the Latin words blazoned across the top. On one side it reads: *Unitati Patriae* (to the unity of the country), and on the opposite side *Libertati Civium* (to the freedom of the citizens).

Since its reopening in 2001, the *Vittoriano* has become one of the most visited attractions in Rome. The climb to the top of the steps is well worth the effort for the **view of the city** which it provides. And if you're willing to buy a ticket for about seven euros you can take an elevator up to the **observation deck** above the columns from where the view is really spectacular. Inside the monument is a permanent museum, *il Museo del Risorgimento*, which illustrates the history of the unification of Italy in the nineteenth century. It also houses many **temporary exhibits** which change periodically.

On the first level, visible from the square below, is the World War I **Tomb of the Unknown Soldier**, whose remains were transferred here in **1921**. The tomb is flanked by perpetually burning torches and two military honor guards. There is a change of the guard every thirty minutes and they are present twenty-four hours a day, even in the worst of weather. The presence of the tomb makes the monument a **sacred place**, and in fact, it is often referred to by Italians as the *Altare della Patria* (Altar of the Fatherland).

A curiosity

• The most prominent decoration on the monument is the enormous **bronze equestrian statue** of Victor Emmanuel II, which is **sixteen times life-size**. If you can imagine this, the horse is so large that after it was set up, a dinner was served **inside its belly** to **twenty-one workers** who represented all those who had labored over the years to build the monument!

Looking down at the *Vittoriano* from a hot-air balloon.

SELECTED BIBLIOGRAPHY

Augias, Corrado. *I Segreti di Roma*. Arnoldo Mondadori. Milano. 2005.

Bruschini, Enrico. *In the Footsteps of Popes*. HarperCollins Publishers. New York. 2001.

Claridge, Amanda. *An Oxford Archaeological Guide: Rome*. Oxford University Press. Oxford. 1998.

Dudley, Donald R. *Urbs Roma*. Phaidon Press. Great Britain. 1967.

Geffcken, Katherine A. and Goldman, Norma W., editors. *The Janus View*. Mundus Media. Clawson, MI. 2007.

Lopez, Antonino. *I Papi*. Futura Edizioni. Roma. 2005.

Macadam, Alta. *City Guide: Rome*. A & C Black. London. 2000.

McBrien, Richard P. *Lives of the Popes*. HarperCollins Publishers. New York. 2000.

McBrien, Richard P. *Lives of the Saints*. HarperCollins Publishers. New York. 2001.

Morrissey, Jake. *The Genius in the Design*. HarperCollens Publishers. New York. 2005.

Paradisi, Donatella. *Calendario di Roma dal 750 a.C. a oggi*. Rendina Editori. Roma. 2000.

Rendina, Claudio, ed. *Enciclopedia di Roma*. Newton & Compton Editori. Roma. 2005.

Rendina, Claudio and Paradisi, Donatella. *La Grande Guida Delle Strade di Roma*. Newton & Compton editori. Roma. 2003.

Scotti, R. A. *Basilica*. Penguin Group. New York. 2006.

Tagliaferri, Alberto and Varriale, Valerio. *Le Strade del mistero di Roma*. Newton Compton editori. Roma. 2006.

ACKNOWLEDGMENTS

Thanks to **Gianfranco Mandas**, my Italian editor, for bringing to life my ideas for the front and back cover, for his priceless assistance in the final arrangement of text and photos, and for the use of many of his own extraordinary photos.

Thanks to **Breck Trevino** for her tireless efforts in the preliminary organization and placing of the photos in the book, as well as for her great patience in helping me to become a little more computer literate.

Thanks to **Karen Hammerlof** who selflessly gave hours of her vacation time in Rome to help proofread the preliminary manuscript for this book.

Thanks to **Paul Canonici**, not only for writing the Foreword of the book, but also for his encouragement and advice along the way.

Thanks to **Shirley Herbert** who has put her considerable journalistic skills to work in proofreading not only the *Sights of Rome* emails over the years, but also the final version of the book.

Thanks to **Warren Caire**, a *Sights* reader from the beginning, who has consistently encouraged me to publish them in book form.

Thanks to **Brett Vogt** for his invaluable help in setting up and monitoring the *Sights of Rome* e-mail group.

Thanks to **my family** back in the U.S.A. for their understanding of my decision to live my life on the other side of the Atlantic.

Thanks to **all the readers of the *Sights* e-mails** for allowing me to flood their mailboxes with my writings over the past few years.

Index

NOTE: Page numbers in bold represent photos.